H OI POLLOI recounts a childl[...]
in bars, as the narrator's pare[...]
ladder. Acclaimed as an 'instant cl[...]
written with extraordinary sympat[...]
finds fresh and hilarious things to say about growing up.

C RAIG SHERBORNE is a former Wal Cherry Play of the Year
award-winner, and winner of the 2008 Queensland Prize for
Non-Fiction for *Muck*. His journalism and poetry have appeared
in most of Australia's leading literary journals and anthologies. He
lives in Melbourne.

'As a writer of memoirs myself, it disturbs me
to admit that Craig Sherborne goes deeper than
the rest of us into the territory of impressionable
immaturity. He writes beautifully, especially
when the material is not beautiful at all. He can
make the cruel truth poetic.'

CLIVE JAMES

PRAISE FOR CRAIG SHERBORNE

'Sherborne has an extraordinary eye for the damage, trivial and profound, that humans inflict on one another ... He has a genius for the telling detail'
LITERARY REVIEW

'Sherborne has recreated the child's-eye view masterfully but just when you think he is making his parents – particularly his mother – a laughing-stock, he turns it back on himself, or conjures a passage of quiet, redemptive beauty'
SYDNEY MORNING HERALD

'A work of searing originality and part of an ongoing masterpiece'
THE MONTHLY

'Craig Sherborne's daring, innovative prose is as exhilarating as his disciplined mastery of it is humbling ... It enlivens us to the comedy, the pathos, the dignity and the pain of life, as his characters live it'
RAIMOND GAITA, author of *Romulus, My Father*

'A lyrical, candid memoir ... Sherborne's parents are reanimated as tragi-comic grotesques, irresistibly awful, touchingly ludicrous, mordantly sensitive and painfully funny'
THE TIMES on *Muck*

HOI POLLOI

First published by Black Inc.

First published in Great Britain 2010 by
Old Street Publishing Ltd
40 Bowling Green Lane, London EC1R 0NE
www.oldstreetpublishing.co.uk

ISBN 978-1-906964-08-5

10 9 8 7 6 5 4 3 2 1

A CIP catalogue record for this title is available from the British
Library.

Printed and bound in Great Britain

HOI POLLOI

A MEMOIR

CRAIG SHERBORNE

THE FIRST TIME I SEE DRUNKS beat up my father I'm six and standing at the bend in the stairs. I press my face against my mother's waist but with one eye I watch as they headlock him from behind at reception because he's ordered them out of his pub. He flails punches, thuds and crunches on their skin, and sinks to one knee. They kick his head. They wear black lace-up bikie boots that have no laces. The police always take so long to come. When they arrive the damage is already done. Sometimes just a nick over his eyebrow. Sometimes a lot more blood and an ambulance is called. He always refuses to go to hospital. He has a lie-down then goes back to work.

We live in Heritage, New Zealand. It's 1968. There are other hotels in Heritage but ours is in the middle of the town, on the main street, Tui Street, and wears the town's name as if more important than the others. My mother likes that. "We're the one that really counts. And don't dare call it a pub, it's such a common word. It's a hotel." I call her Heels just for using to myself. I call my father Winks. You can work out why.

In walking terms Heritage is ten minutes long by eight or so wide. It has a rail line running north–south through greeny-brown farm hills. People generally keep it neat with swept driveways and white paint on the ironwork atop their fences. But on the other side of town there are khaki brick and weatherboard places Heels calls "commission boxes" and indeed they are like boxes, I see for myself when Winks drives us through there but never to visit. Heels says you can tell when people own their houses because of the gardens. They keep their ironwork all spruced up and grow hydrangeas up high as the roof. They care more. People who rent don't care.

We live in an apartment over the public bar where men say fuck at the top of their voices and if I put my ear to the floor I can hear them. An apartment like fancy folk do in Paris and New York, Heels says. It's becoming fashionable as well across the ditch in Sydney. Not a flat, an *apartment*. I can reach out of my bedroom window and not quite touch the town clock's hands. The clock chimes the hours off through the night but I'm used to it and only half-wake at the hammer-on-metal tolling. Sometimes it becomes part of any dream I'm dreaming.

I hate Heritage. Heels tells me to. She says it will set me up for later in life. It will help me aim for better things and never settle for Heritage. Here there are no fine shops, the clothes shops are dreadful and the air tastes of chemical taint from the spray from outlying orchards. She says the population is meant to be 50,000 but they're pulling our leg and it's more like half that number. Besides, you wouldn't bother with more than ten of them.

Rugby teams come to stay and throw their mattresses

from the windows for a drunken dare. *Our* mattresses because they're owned by us and not by some footballer. Let them treat their own mattresses that way.

There are many horis in Heritage with their hori ways and foul mouths always complaining about the beer being flat and the pool table on a slant. Hori is the pakeha put-down name for Maori. It sounds about the same as Maori, no better no worse, but it's a word you don't say out loud to Maoris. It's for using among ourselves. Pakeha sounds like a Maori put-down for whites. It's pronounced with a swear-like *puk* at the start which rhymes with fuck and couldn't help but come out of your mouth with a few bits of spit. But it seems to be a proper, respectful word. Even Heels and Winks use it and aren't offended. "Give them a chance and the horis will take us over," say the pakehas. They complain that it's already begun, this taking over because horis are worming their way into the English language with an ugly word like pakeha and pakehas are using it every day as if it were their own and not even thinking twice about doing it.

There's the big Goodes cannery in town. Sir Thomas Goodes started the factory many years ago in his garage just up the road in Hay Street and look at him now. Some nights he parks his black Bentley outside our front door, the hotel front door, and pops in for a drink. Heels loves it when he does this. Such a gentleman in his dark suit and shiny brogue shoes. Such a tonic to the horis with their singlets and "box of match, Mrs." Horis use filthy language in front of her and one time spat directly at her and another time tried to grope her privates and made her weep and feel like a common bar-maid. Whenever I wear my cap-gun outfit I shoot horis in my room, make them suffer for treating Heels and Winks this way with their beatings and groping and spitting. I use piles of guest laundry outside in the hall to punch them and spit at them back.

Heels sighs that it's impossible to feel special in Heritage. It's impossible to be any good where there are commission houses and horis. Even Sir Thomas Goodes who has a Bentley and can afford anything is reduced to doing his socialising here among *them*. "Among us too," I comfort her. But she says, "We're outnumbered." Not even racehorses make you special here. In Heritage every pakeha and not a few horis have one, any old farmer or tradesman or you name it. They train them themselves at the Heritage racecourse or in farm paddocks for goodness' sake and don't even pay a pretty sum for them but breed them from some relative's back-paddock mare and are a dime a dozen.

In Australia it's different. You must be wealthy and *be* somebody to own a racehorse in Australia, it's a sign of success. When Heels and Winks talk about Australia they always include "We love it over there" in a sentence and "It's going ahead in leaps and bounds" and "There are no horis to speak of, they dealt with theirs." They have lots of holidays in Australia. I was born in Sydney on one such holiday, a boasting point for Heels who's fond of saying "of course, my son was born in Sydney" in a way that means I'm a cut above Heritage and she is too because she can afford to go there and because of that she knows what's *in* and what's *out*. *In* for a lady is to have your hair swept up, the whole works, into a bun and tinted peach or apricot and sprayed stiff till it's 100 per cent wind-proof. Slacks and sandals are *the* thing over there and bright flowery blouses and sunglasses with gold, curly frames, and false nails, long and red-pink. Matching colour on your toes, and a ruby necklace. All other jewellery should be gold at all times. *Real* gold. Rings, real diamonds. Gold in your teeth is out, that's for peasants. It's all porcelain now. Everyone's getting their top teeth pulled out because a person's smile is their passport, white, perfect.

I, however, am not perfect: it is disappointing that I have a stutter. But we're working on it. Each Thursday after school I cycle to Mrs Daley for elocution lessons, sputtering out a recital of poems ...

I must go down to the seas again, to the lonely seas and the sky,
And all I ask is a tall ship and star to steer her by.

... with the same exaggerated mouth movements Mrs Daley makes as she pushes her pinkie through wires of a budgie cage and lets the yellow bird bite her nail.

I'm left-handed which must also be cured because it makes me look deformed when I write, my wrist twisted in a horrible fashion over the page. Left-handedness is for half-wits, therefore Heels ties a piece of string on my left index finger. Whenever I lower my head to write I will see the string and pass the pen to my right hand. If she sees me writing with my left hand again I'll be smacked.

Heels likes me to dress in my Sydney clothes, my walk-socks and bow-tie with the Grace Brothers label. Or in winter a collarless coat made of long animal hair, a goat maybe, shimmery-silver with plaited leather buttons. The coat's from Surfers Paradise, she tells the bar staff and the cleaners and guest-room maids. Surfers where? they ask.

"Surfers Paradise."

"There's a place called Paradise?"

"There certainly is."

"Where?"

"Queensland."

"Where's that exactly?"

"Plllease," Heels rolls her eyes at their ignorance.

A Mercedes Benz is special. A Mercedes Benz 250. No one else in Heritage has a Mercedes. One cannot even buy a Mercedes in Heritage. One has to ring a car dealer in Auckland. The dealer will order a brochure from the Mercedes people in Sydney and Heels and Winks can select a model. A Mercedes is so special it will take six months to arrive from Germany, which lost the war. Maroon with white upholstery. In preparation for the big day Heels buys Winks a leather driving glove for Christmas, ordered by phone from Sydney. Winks orders Heels a snazzy headscarf for travelling. Heels rings her brother in the South Island. He inherited the family butcher business because he was the only son and therefore had the birthright when Granddad died. Till now he's done better than her in life but now *she's* buying a Mercedes. She rings her sister who owns a motel her husband built with his own hands. They buy a new Jaguar every two years because they don't have children. But a Jaguar is no Mercedes.

Heels is looking forward to driving me to school. I don't look forward to it though. I dread it. I don't want to stand out like someone would who's driven to school in a Mercedes. I have trouble fitting in as it is. "It's not mine it's my parents'," I'll have to plead.

Winks agrees with me, I shouldn't have to wear the goat-hair coat to school. "It's very stylish for Heritage," he tells Heels and winks to me that he's on my side. I'm already sniggered at for my bow-tie and walk-socks and brown leather Sydney shoes. "Lost puppy," the boys shout while I sit by myself eating my cheese and jam sandwiches. When I take off my shoes and socks for lunchtime bullrush my feet are narrow and so spotlessly white they're transparent to the veins. The other boys have wide brown feet, hard and dirty with toenails missing and sores on their ankles. They only choose people with feet like their own for their sides.

Heels is adamant: "I won't have him visiting Sir Thomas Goodes looking like riff-raff. He will wear his goat-hair coat." But I'm not visiting Sir Thomas Goodes. I'm going on a school excursion to the Goodes cannery, I tell her. I'm going to observe how they process vegetables. But Heels raises her voice that she doesn't care whether it's a school excursion or not, put on the goat coat and do as you're told you ungrateful so-and-so. "If I'm going to accompany you, you'll look smart in my presence."

Heel has volunteered to be a parent helper at the excursion. She never does that sort of thing. She did not, I suspect, volunteer simply to be a helper. She wants to size up the class, the girl named Sandra I've been caught watching pee in the girls' toilet. Sandra invited me to. She invited all the boys in the class into the girls' toilet. She pulled up her skirt, pulled her white undies down and sat astride the bowl facing us and peed out through the bare mound with a split in it between her legs she showed was her cuntie. She said we could touch her pee as it came out the split and then poke a finger up inside her as far as it could go before hurting. It smelt watery sour.

I felt excitement doing this, excitement that wasn't the normal kind that made me run about. I was standing absolutely still. The bag of puffy skin below my cocko shrivelled and prickled. We touched her pee, put in a finger and agreed to pee in front of her and let her put her finger under the stream. But after I pulled down my pants, going second after Damien, aiming to pee on top of Sandra's and Damien's pee while Sandra sat on the cistern to watch, Mrs Quigley walked in. "Stop it. Stop it at once," she yelled, clapping her hands to hurry us out of there, clipping me across the back of my head as I ran doing up my zipper.

She rang the parents of the children involved. That night Heels was in a rage. When she's in a rage her eyes flare open to their whites. Her jaw juts forward till her yellow real bottom teeth overbite her false clean top ones. She sucks the air like a person about to lift something heavy. She flexes her fingers, scratching the air with her red nails. That night she was able to speak. Sometimes she's too involved in her rage to speak, but that night her sucking and scratching produced a question as she circled me. "What can you tell me about this girl, this Sandra?" When she hates something she puts "this" before its name. "Is she a hori? I heard her grandfather had hori in him." She nodded to herself the way she does when she's about to say, "I should've known." And that's what she did say. "I should've known. The little slut's a hori."

Winks spoke up from outside the circle she was walking: "Language, love. Slut's strong stuff."

She didn't acknowledge his presence. She said she refused to believe that a child of hers would be involved in such filth. She demanded the heavens tell her why there are no private schools in Heritage. Someone should have started a decent school and I could have gone there. She made Winks take his belt from his waist and stand by with it looped into a whip. She told me to list everyone who was in the toilet at the time of the disgusting episode.

I began with Damien. Heels shook her head. "Damien's father is a respected orchardist. They've just built a house. You expect me to believe Damien was a part of this depravity?" Next was Peter. She shook her head again. "The accountant chappy's boy? I won't believe that." Next, I said Tamoa. Heels slapped her hands on her knees: "I knew it. I knew it. A hori would be in this. I bet he was the ring-leader." She softened her voice. "Is that right, dear?" I gave her the answer she wanted: "Yes." She sighed. She smiled at me, kissed my forehead. She said I could not possibly under-stand how embarrassed she and my father were, in their posi-tion as leading business people in Heritage, with a son who associates with horis. Winks threaded his belt around his trousers. Heels was still smiling and talking softly. I felt it was a good time to speak up. "B-b-but *you* m-m-mix w-with h-h-horis." Heels' eyes widened to their full whites again. Winks stopped threading his belt. I said, "H-here. In the h-h-hotel. Th-they're in h-here all th-th-the time." Heels let out a scoffing breath. So did Winks. "That's business, dear," she said. "They come in here. We take their money. And we're glad to see the back of them until tomorrow. It's a prof-itable business or else we wouldn't put up with them."

Heels says horis are not like pahekas in the following ways: they are drunkards, uncouth, violent, that's their natu-ral state of behaviour, look at what they do to your father, they're nothing but animals.

I've also noticed they have missing teeth but wear no dentures like pakehas. They are twice as big as pakehas except very big pakehas. They are brown even in winter, a dappled bruise-blue brown. They have much thicker arms and legs, and noses and lips. Their eyes are closer together on their face. They laugh with a high-pitched giggle but have deep voices. Though they speak English it sounds low and growling as if they're really speaking Hori but are speaking English at the same time. Pakehas have red, black and blue tattoos of snakes and knives, curvy women in tight dresses, anchors and flames. Horis have faded blue handwriting tattoos, including on their fingers, *Love*, *Mum*, *Hate*, *Death* like the tattoos Tamoa scratches into himself at playtimes with a safety pin and ink bottle. Horis have runny noses like Tamoa. I have a runny nose in winter but *they* have them all the time. I use a handkerchief, white or chequered and ironed into a square. Hori children use their thumb and tongue. They go barefoot and wear rugby shorts in all weather or workman shorts that are too baggy. They have long strips of skin on the end of their cockos and pakehas have none.

"The things they do to their women," Heels says with a shudder. "Belt them and make them do terrible things."

"What things?" I ask.

"Never you mind. Terrible things."

Terrible things. She also says that about Mr Chipperfield, and Mr Chipperfield is a pakeha and works at the bus company a few doors down on Tui Street. Mr Chipperfield does terrible things, she says, you are not to talk to him anymore.

"Why not?"

"Just don't."

"Why not?"

"He likes children."

I like Mr Chipperfield. Mr Chipperfield always has time to wonder aloud, How are you? Come and sit down and tell old Chips what you've been up to.

"Mr Chipperfield's *like* is not *like* in the usual way. He has never asked you to do things, has he?"

"What things?"

"To go for a drive in his car?"

"Yes."

"He has?"

"Yes. Into the countryside."

"Oh God, the bastard. You must never, ever speak to him again. He likes to do things to children. To touch them. And for them to touch him. Did he ever ask you to do that?"

"Yes."

"The bastard. What exactly did he ask? To hold him, down *there*? His John Thomas?"

"Yes."

"And did you?"

"I was going to but a bus drove in and Mr Chipperfield had to go."

"You must never ever touch anyone's John Thomas but your own."

"What terrible things do horis do to their women? As terrible as Mr Chipperfield's things?"

"The same. Worse. Oh for God's sake, what a dreadful topic."

*

The grade is told to form two lines for the excursion and hold hands with the next child. Everyone except me is shivering in the morning chill, pulling their jumper arms over their fists. It's quite an occasion going to Goodes cannery. Tamoa and the horis are wearing shoes. Shoes that flop on them too big and don't look right without socks. I'm wearing the goat coat and pretend to shiver, sniffle and cough so the coat might seem a lesser thing in Heels' eyes and pointless to have forced me to wear it. She's dressed like always as if going out to a ball. Her face is pale with powder. Her hair, tinted blond with a pink haze through it, is swirled into a cone. She wears a white trench coat over her blue frock, her favourite frock that goes down to near her ankles. Around her neck there's the stole she likes to show people is mink from George Street, Sydney. Her high heels are less high than usual because she has a long walk ahead of her, but high all the same.

Everyone wants to touch and stroke the goat coat. Their lips are pursed holding back laughter. They don't want to hold hands with me and I become proud and say I don't want to hold hands with them either. I stand with my chin pointing up in the air and make it plain that at least I'm warm and not shivering and chattering my teeth like them. I even hold my breath so no mist will escape from my mouth. Sandra touches the coat, pulls its hair-ends out to their full length and snorts a small laugh with her fingers up to her mouth. But she also takes my hand to walk off, out of the school playground, across town to Goodes.

Heels puts her hands on my shoulder and pulls me away from Sandra until our grip breaks. She marches me down the line looking for a suitable hand. Tamoa's hand is free but she pushes past him and past the hori girl Bronwyn, and another hori girl, Aroha. "There seem to be no free hands," she says to Mrs Quigley and pushes me a little further towards the front where Damien is holding hands with Leeanne Brightways, her with the lovely yellow hair plaited down her back like so much fine rope. Heels breaks their grip and puts Leeanne's hand and mine together and tells Damien to hold hands with Leeanne's twin sister, Adele, who's standing right behind and has rope hair as well. The boy Adele is holding hands with has to hold hands with whoever is behind him. On it goes down the lines until the holding hands matter is settled and we all file up the street in a cloud of breathing. Tamoa holds hands with Sandra.

The factory clatters and wheezes like a giant car engine. Workers wear white overalls and caps. They smooth labels onto cans with a quick roll of the hand and send the cans away on conveyor belts. The factory manager gives a speech about how the company began in a cottage in Ranfurly Street more than thirty years ago and at first only turned out 20,000 cans a day but it's twenty times that now. It makes $60 million a year. Heels gasps at the figure. Mrs Quigley follows her lead and gasps. Everybody begins gasping repeatedly until hushed. The manager holds out a plate of raw greens for us to sample. String beans, peas, broadbeans puffy in their pods. At the hotel it used to be Tia's job to shell these things and cook them. She made me milkshakes and gingerbreads in between shellings while I sat in the kitchen near the door with a round window in it for waitresses to peep through before carrying out steaks to the dining room.

Tia often did something secretive as she worked behind saucepans at the bench. She slipped a handful of greens into her apron pocket. Sometimes she did the same with lumps of butter or a rasher of bacon wrapped in a paper serviette. She emptied her apron pocket into her flax carry bag. I wondered why on earth she did this—why be so secretive about a handful of beans and some butter? But I said nothing to her because it was obvious she never intended me to notice. One night I asked Heels what Tia might do with the food in her apron pocket. I certainly didn't mean to get Tia into trouble over a few beans, but Heels sucked and scratched the air in that way she does and said, "I'll put her on notice tomorrow."

Winks shrugged that that's probably wise. "It's not as if we don't pay the woman."

"Horis are hopeless with money," said Heels.

"I thought she was a good one."

Tia made no more milkshakes or gingerbreads. She turned the radio on whenever I tried to talk to her. If she'd have done this only once, maybe twice, it wouldn't have hurt me so. But through the next week my hurt hardened to resentment that she should ignore me over and over. How dare she refuse to speak to me. What makes her think she can treat me this way. She should be grateful to have the son of the people who hire her want to talk to her at all and keep her company. I began to see how blue and swollen her ankles were, how red her fingers. She had dots of sweat in her curly black hair and ugly black hairs coming out the tops of her toes. She smelt too, a man's sweating smell. I no longer wanted to be near her unless it was to bring a book into the kitchen, those thick thrillers Winks keeps by the bed, and pretend I could read it fast, nodding and smiling as if the story amused me. Tia couldn't read or write, she once told me. Surely she watched me enviously. Surely she was thinking how I'd grow up to do a job that involved lots of reading the way important people do, while she would stay a cook, a hori cook.

One day she never turned up for work in the morning. She never turned up again. Heels said that was typical of horis.

I take a pea pod from the factory manager's plate and cut it open with my fingernail for eating. Tamoa selects a string bean. He turns it in his hand like a brilliant stone, stares at it, blinks. Heels is over talking to Mrs Quigley so I move closer to Tamoa. "Haven't you eaten a bean before?" I ask him, meaning it as a joke not a question.

"No," he says.

I have to laugh at that and Tamoa glares at me and calls the bean fucking pakeha shit. Pippies, puha from the roadside and the mussels his relations get from the beach, that's *his* kind of food, he says. Sometimes lamb when someone has a hangi. Lamb was pakeha food too, but not when cooked as a hangi. Aroha tells Tamoa to shut up because the reason he didn't eat beans is because his parents don't have enough money for food after they've paid for beer. She says she's had beans and peas for years because her father has a job at the freezing works. He can buy and steal good meat whenever he wants.

Tamoa bites into the bean and spits it into Aroha's face, cursing "Fucking pakeha shit" loud enough that Mrs Quigley hears and the manager frowns. Heels and Mrs Quigley walk this way so I turn my back on Tamoa.

*

The first day Heels drives me to school in the new Mercedes I tell her I want to vomit. No, not car sickness. Embarrassment.

"Don't you dare be sick in this car," she hisses, her jaw starting to jut, the sucking sound starting to come out of her mouth. She tells me I should be grateful to be able to travel in such comfort to school. I should appreciate it and be proud of how hard she and Winks have worked and slaved to afford such a nice thing as a Mercedes Benz because when she was a girl she never had such luxuries. She had to walk to school five miles through a Christchurch winter to go to school when *she* was a girl. What she wouldn't have given to be chauffeured in a Mercedes like a little lord. Even going to school was a luxury in her day. She draws breath. Juts and sucks. She reminds me that Winks had to leave school when he was eleven because his own father, my grandfather, was such a no-hoper. He had some get up and go, your father, she says. Imagine, eleven, working—dangerous timber yards, gravel quarries, with nothing for dinner but a single roast potato. And here you are complaining about being driven to school in a beautiful Mercedes.

I hate the car. I'm scared to move in case my shoes put nugget on the white leather. People stare at me from the street. I can no longer go to school in private but with eyes following me like a celebrity. I ask Heels if from now on I can walk to school like she herself had done on those bitter winter mornings.

"If that's the way you feel then walk to school. That's gratitude for you," she juts. She pulls the car over, reaches across and opens my door. It's my cue to say I'm sorry and not get out of the car. I bow my head. I say I'm sorry.

We arrive at the school gate as morning bell sounds and skipping and hopscotch paths are being deserted. I carefully shuffle out of the car without scuffing anything. "Kiss," demands Heels as usual, cocking her cheek for me. I lean across and peck her. "That's pretty weak," she says as usual. I kiss her again with more force and hold my breath so as not to inhale her makeup and perfume which blend into a smell that's metallic-tasting and makes my eyes burn and run until I sneeze. As soon as I'm out on the pavement free of her I wipe away the coating of face powder kissing her always leaves on my lips. I run-walk from the car hoping not to be associated with it.

Tamoa stands up from where he's been crouched behind the for-climbing-up tree. He steals his father's cigarettes and hides them in the trunk there. He stares at the Mercedes as it drives off, his mouth wide open. "Hey, *e hoa*," he says. *E hoa* is Maori for friend but can be used in a threatening way because it sounds threatening pronounced *air whore*. Tamoa uses it that way. He calls everyone *e hoa*. "That a Rolls Royce?" he asks.

"No, it's a Mercedes."

"Oh," he grunts, suddenly unimpressed. He has a smoking butt in his curled-up fingers and sucks on it as if chewing his nails. He then stubs it out beneath his bare big toe and stows it in the for-climbing-up tree.

I begin walking to the classroom but stop because I want to ask Tamoa something. He's a good person to ask because for one thing he's older than me. Not in years, we're both eight, but older in other ways—his smoking, his tattoos, his disobedience in class. His saying he's finished with school and won't come back next year. To Tamoa school is for pakehas. One day the pakehas will all be killed if they're not careful, he says. The Maoris will run things. "So you better be a friend of mine *e hoa*, or else," he says and runs his finger across his throat like a knife.

For another thing, Tamoa's a hori, and my question requires a hori to answer it. There are two questions on my mind in fact. One: is *pakeha* a hori swear word about people who aren't hori? Two: what things do hori men do to women? I don't say the word *hori* to him though.

His answer to question number one on the word *pakeha* is, No, it's a good word, not like *hori* for example. Tamoa says the word *hori* in his sentence but I act as if I've never heard it before. As for question two about hori men and what they do to women, Tamoa says he has no idea. His father gives his mother a belting sometimes, but that's normal, isn't it? Your dad does that to your mother, doesn't he?, he asks. Yes of course he does, I lie.

I'm about to walk into class when Tamoa slaps my arm—in a friendly way, not for fighting. "Onions," he says. "My cousin talks about onions and women." But that's all he knows about it because his cousin is trying to get into the Mongrel Mob and the onions are to do with them but they're a secret, not to be blabbed outside the gang, especially to pakehas. He asks me why I want to know. I tell him that my mother talks about it and therefore it must be important.

*

I'm too spoilt and that's the reason I can't sleep, Heels decides. I should get used to the rowdy voices from down in the bars. I should ignore the glasses being smashed outside on the footpath and the yelling as people go home. "Do you think *I* like it? No, I do not," she complains and wants me to know she has to put a cold flannel on her eyes and over her forehead to relax and block it all out. So I'm not to go thinking I'm the only one, think about *her* for a change. No I certainly cannot have a baby bottle of milk like I sometimes do, I'm eight years old now and no son of hers is going to act like a bloody baby. No more baby bottle with a teat on it to relax me to sleep. She doesn't care if I am afraid of the smashed glasses and yelling, a baby's bottle is out of the question. But all right then, if I can't sleep I'm to come downstairs and make myself useful. Go into the Private Bar and unstack the glasses from the washer trays and place them for drying, upside down, on the drying rack.

The Private Bar is what she calls *couth*. Men must wear ties. Sir Thomas Goodes, when he parks his Bentley out front, sits in the corner of the Private Bar reading the newspaper. "Stout as usual, Sir Thomas?" Heels enquires, bringing him a Heritage Hotel coaster with a red sketch of the Hotel printed on it.

My school headmaster, Mr Atkinson, sits in another corner filling his pipe and then sucking out the smoke. His drink is whisky and milk. There's suave Charlie Carmichael, that's what Heels calls him, *suave*, with his blond wavy hair at fifty. He also drinks whisky and milk, with a bit of ice. Drinkers sit at laminex tables or the sticky towelled counter. No uncouth liquor like beer is drunk in the Private Bar. People drink the classier, expensive drinks—the wine, brandy, whisky or ports. They say "lovely" and make a smacking sound with their lips after the first sip while smoke comes out of their nostrils like streamers. Women are allowed to drink in the Private Bar. They are *not* allowed to drink in the Public Bar, but can go into the Lounge Bar if accompanied by a male. Horis are allowed anywhere by law, but fortunately, whispers Heels, they don't come into the Private Bar because of the tie rule. The Salvation Army is forbidden to enter the premises. They'll put us out of business with their tin rattling and teetotalling nonsense.

Charlie Carmichael smokes Rothmans with the fancy, swirly writing on the pack and speckled brown filter. His lighter's silver. He bought it in Sydney. "Ah, of course, you can tell something as stylish as that would hail from Sydney," Heels says. "Best not to mention Sydney or I'll get depressed

I'm here not there." He can flick his lighter open, light up a cigarette and snap the lighter shut in less than a second, a record for anyone in the hotel. I've timed them.

He trains Winks and Heels' three racehorses (two wins and a third) and if he could establish himself with a few winners in Sydney he'd be there for good in a shot. "It's the big time," he insists, putting his hand flat on the bar like a slow smack. He drinks till he's just sober enough for Winks to help him by the arm to wobble to his car and make sure he can start it and doesn't fall asleep with his head on the horn instead. Heels won't hear of him being called a boozer by Winks or anyone else. As far as she's concerned he's a civilised drinker with Sydney ambitions. Yes, he may like to get tipsy at night, but when have you ever heard of him not getting up at five every morning to work his horses? That's the definition of a civilised drinker: they get up in the morning and do their work. Unlike the horis. That's why the police only book horis. Pakehas get a warning because if they lost their licence they wouldn't be able to drive to work. Isn't that right, Senior Sergeant?

"You've hit the nail on the proverbial head, madam," belly-laughs the Senior Sergeant, placing a shiny wood-pole, his nightstick, on the bar. He says he has time for a quick one. He turns a blind eye to us staying open later than Closing. Each month he receives two dozen flagons of draught as a gesture.

After Closing I help empty ashtrays and collect dirty glasses from the tables. "Lovely," I mimic, sniffing the whisky tumblers. I swirl the near-melted ice at the bottom. The smell is sickly-sweet and sour all at once. Why would people want to drink this?

I wait till no one is near, no one looking, and duck under the bar-flap with a tray of dirty glasses. I take the tray into the phone box beside the stairs, close the door, crouch down below its glass window so as not to be seen. I sit on the sticky carpet to sip the dregs. Cold and watery but with soft-drink and cough-syrup flavours. I eat the ice lumps and suck up the liquid. I think I'll only take a minute more but I lose track of time. I try to stand but have to sit straight back down. My cheeks have gone hot and there is a pleasant-unpleasant sense of the floor being uneven. My stomach rises into my throat. I might throw up any second. I'm sure I will, but the moment passes. Sleep. I have to go to sleep now.

I make it out the door and climb the stairs the slowest I have ever climbed them. Next night I sneak another tray into the phone box. And the next. And the next. A week. Two weeks of it. I sleep heavily, blackly. There's barely a dream I can remember. I'm sluggish in the mornings—it's impossible to get out of bed for school which Heels and Winks put down to a growth spurt. Sometimes they let me stay home and sleep all day because of the growth spurts.

WHEN THE APARTMENT PHONE rings after eight at night it means trouble. "Horis again, Dad?"

September Sixth. The Spring Blossom Festival. The orchards are blooming in Heritage. Row on row of tree reds, whites, purples on the outskirts of town. The crossways rains have finished. My jumper can come off by midday. Clouds stretch out in strips so thin you can see straight through them. The festival is tradition. We must respect tradition, we are told at school. Every year since World War II floats edge their way down Tui Street, stuck with real and paper blossom. Men in clown costumes toss Macintosh lollies to the crowd. Children dressed as fairies dance on the floats and bless the crowd with tinfoil wands. Even the hori gangs get blessed—the Mongrel Mob and Black Power from all over the North Island. This morning, as they do every Spring Festival, they arrive crammed in old cars with pink door panels and missing bumpers, or ride snorting motorbikes with long banana-bike handlebars. The police are still negotiating where they can park. They can't park in the street, it will block the parade. This is a happy occasion please boys, no one wants any strife. Park off Tui Street next to the railway line. OK, motorbikes, motorbikes only, can stay here, but on the footpath so they don't block the floats, not out in the street.

I lean out my bedroom window. The Senior Sergeant's blue bobby helmet is nodding down below. Other bobby helmets nod around him. Black curly heads nod back: "Here for a good time is all boss." An arm lifts up and wants to rest on the Senior Sergeant's shoulder. It's a denim arm with frayed, grimy cuffs. The Senior Sergeant slowly pushes the arm away and holds his hands up to stop any more denim arms being placed around his shoulders. "Here for a good time is all boss."

On the denim backs are skull and cross-bone patches with tongues poking out of the skull. Winks is also down there standing near the Senior Sergeant. He's saying he doesn't want a repeat of past years. He wants the hotel entrance to be clear at all times for patrons. He tries to touch a denim shoulder but his hand is shrugged away. "Here for a good time is all boss."

A black curly head bends back to drink from a beer bottle. "No drinking in the street," say the bobby helmets.

"Not drinking in the street boss. Drinking on the footpath."

Denim arms try but fail to offer bobby helmets a swig. "Too fucking good to drink with us?"

Come the night, Heels is crying. She says she's sick of this life. The hori gangs are behaving like animals downstairs. That's all they are, animals. But what can we do? Ban them and they start a fight. Let them into the bars and they start a fight. This festival good for the town? Utter rubbish.

A cultural event? A joke. The bars are full but so what, count up the damage at the end of the night—glasses, windows, stools, toilet doors, God knows what else. Count that up and say Spring Festival is good for business. Not to mention the cash we've forked out to footballers to become bouncers for the night. Sell up and move to Sydney before there's nothing left to sell because of those animals down there. Sell up and move to Sydney. "I never want to see another hori again," she sniffles.

Winks lies in his clothes on the bed beside her. He rests his arm across his eyes. The air stinks of the bar-smoke on him. What if Winks was ever killed by the animals? Don't the horis think about that? What would happen to us? To *me*? Don't they care? How dare they not care.

"Are we r-r-really m-m-moving to Sydney?" Winks doesn't answer me. The phone rings. He jumps up and answers that instead. Out he goes through the door. I check the clock: ten to nine. I'm more frightened than usual when the phone rings late. It's Heels' crying. Would she please stop crying! Stop it. Stop. I hop onto her bed. The makeup is melting from her eyes. Normally she wants me to kiss her on the lips and hold the kiss for a while. I hate it and always wriggle away. I try to kiss her now that way to please her but she's not in the mood. She covers her face with her hands.

I want to go to the phone box with a tray of dregs and then sleep, but I couldn't sleep anyway, not with horis gangs down in the foyer. How could I sleep when Winks is dealing with the animals and in such danger. What use am I asleep! I should be alongside him helping him. Helping instead of what I usually do when he's fighting—stand, watch, bawl. I could guard the stairs and shout out if the horis start climbing them. I'm too scared to do a thing like that. No I'm not. Yes I am. I could stand beside him and be brave like him. I could take a weapon. Some baby I'd be then. The knives in the kitchen. If I had one of them then because I'm tall for my age I could reach up and stab a hori in the stomach.

I go to my room. It's beside Heels and Winks' room. Heels is lying on her bed silent now between sobs so I better be quiet pulling my clothes over my pyjamas, doing up my shoes. I put a pillow under the blankets to fake my body. I crawl low on hands and knees so Heels won't notice my shadow pass her door towards the front door which is always locked. I'll have to take the spare key from the hook beside the front door to get back in. Once through the door floorboards creak all the way along the guest hall but who's going to hear my footsteps above the din of bar voices below?

What sort of knife? Choose one. I'm taking too long. I don't really want to go downstairs and help Winks. That's why I'm dilly-dallying here in the kitchen dark. I should choose a knife with a pointy end, the ones with rough sides are good for nothing but bread. I select one with a smooth side and hold it up to the streetlight light shining through the window. This one's good, a bit heavy but pointy. This one is the one to take. I'll name it Sword.

The stairs dog-leg down to the lobby. The bend in the stairs, the part where the stairs become floor for a second, is what I consider the top of the stairs because it's my lookout perch. The swing doors of the Public Bar are directly below and in front of me. The Lounge Bar is off to the right. The phone box is tucked away to the left at the foot of the stairs. Further left is the hotel entrance, the foyer. I crouch behind the stair post. I use my sleeve as a sheath for Sword but the blade is cold and might cut my arm so I slip it under the loose carpet on a step.

"Why no pool cues boss? Can't play pool with no cues boss?" Winks will not put the cues back on the table because they're for pool, not for hitting someone across the head.

"Can't play pool with no cues boss."

Winks tells the hori who's saying this that he has to leave, get out of the hotel, he's not allowed back in the bar. He grabs him by his denim elbow. The hori jerks his elbow free. Winks tells him to get out now or there'll be a carry-on. He tells him he's got to the count of five. He tells two footballers with rolled-up sleeves and dented noses to pick up the motorbike blocking the front door and if its owner won't move it then feel free to throw it into the fucking street. One. Two. Three. Move. Four. Out. Five.

Winks grabs a handful of the denim hori. Should I run down now to help? I pull Sword from the carpet. The denim hori is bigger than Winks but Winks is fast, his aim is good. His blows hit the denim hori's face. The denim hori misses with his fists. Winks' buttons rip off. His shirt hangs out, torn. He tips the denim hori to the floor and a footballer helps him to snatch and yank on denim and hair until the hori has been dragged out the front door while yelling long and wordless.

Two other denim horis barge through the Public Bar swing doors and stomp towards Winks with their fists held up. They call the hori who was just dragged out their brother and shout that Winks is a cunt. Three footballers run out of the Public Bar after them, tackle them to the ground. Winks comes back through the front door, tucking his shirt in, but there's another denim hori behind him who's shaking out a length of thick chain. He's going to swing it at Winks, I can see it coming. I open my mouth and scream "Chain" with all my body but no sound comes out as in a dream when I run but don't get anywhere. My voice is frozen inside me and will not shift. My legs, my fist clenching the knife, are frozen. I push and push but no sound. The chain hits Winks across the neck. Still my voice is frozen. No sound. Winks catches the end of the chain and is tug-of-warring with the horis. My legs are so weak they tremble and are about to buckle under me. I can't help him. I can't make it down there to lend weight on the chain.

"Hey little boss. Look at the little boss." One of them is climbing the stairs. He laughs, head thrown back close enough to me that I see the black holes in his gums from having no front teeth. He gulps from a beer jug and has to grab the balustrade to steady himself. "What you going to do with that knife, little boss?" He is one step from me. Stab him, I roar in my head.

But I haven't stabbed him. I couldn't stab him. I run and he follows up the stairs into the dim-lit guest hall, a shadow man in the dark with a high hori laugh like a boy. "Where are you, little boss?" he calls coming towards the kitchen. I huddle where the sacks of potatoes go under the sink. The heaving breath and tears in me are making too much noise. Surely he'll find me. I no longer hold the knife. Where is it? I don't know where it is. I've dropped it. If he knew I no longer held the knife he might just go away. Has he picked it up for himself?

The kitchen-to-dining room door squeaks open. "Little boss. Little boss."

"Hey. Get out of there. Get out of there." It's Winks' voice getting closer in the hall. The thud and heavy squeak of the door pushed wide. Heavy boots slap across lino. The tap-tap-tap of rawhide soles, Winks' soles, pursues them.

"Hey," Winks bellows. "Hey."

I hear grunts, the thump of hands on bodies trying to grab a hold. The fire-escape door rattles, a pane of glass smashes. Then nothing but the blood-ocean sound of my palms squashing my ears deaf.

I relax my hands and open my eyes. Bar noise from below and the farmy smell of hessian and potato soil seeps into me. A cold draught blows about the floor. I don't want to leave my hiding place but it's becoming chillier here by the second as if inside has suddenly become the outside. My feet have gone to sleep and my legs ache with cramp. I climb out onto my hands and knees and peep around the sink corner for any sign of Winks or the hori. No one. The fire-escape door is ajar and rocking on its hinges from an icy breeze. There—the knife's silvery blade beside the Formica table. I tip-toe to collect it, put it back on the drawer. I run as fast as I can on tip-toes to the apartment, aim the key at the lock with trembling fingers and crawl past Heels and Winks' room. Heels is talking angrily on the phone, "Why has no divvy van arrived yet? We pay our taxes and when we need police you people won't do your job."

I get into bed and lie there, wide awake.

Still wide awake. And now Winks has returned. He's telling Heels something. He's trying to keep his voice down. She talks that way too, not loud enough to be an argument but obviously more important than any argument. I can tell in their whispery voices a great worry, a panic. I slip out of bed, cup my hands to my ears and press against their door. She's saying, "Leave him there" and "It will look like a fall."

He says, "I'm in trouble with this one. Jesus."

"We should drag him off the premises. Turf him into the street."

"You think?"

She keeps asking him the same question—"What exactly happened?"—and he keeps giving the same answer and wishing it could be different. He keeps saying, "It was a lucky punch. It was a lucky punch."

I've worked out what they're doing. They're making a plan. It's to do with the denim hori who was in the kitchen. Winks has punched him and the denim hori has fallen backwards down the fire-escape, all those steel steps, and he's dead. Dead. He's lying on the concrete where he landed and not breathing, not moving, and there's no pulse. Maybe the police will treat it as a robbery, Winks says. The hori was drunk and lost his balance in the act of burglary.

"Drag him off the premises," Heels repeats. "Deny any knowledge. For Christ's sake, you could go to jail otherwise," she says in a hushed shout.

Jail? How could Winks ever go to jail? The denim hori was a hori. Horis go to jail. Pakehas don't go to jail. Winks has his jobs to do in the morning, he's a busy man. He's my father and can't be taken away. But what about Mr Chipperfield? He wasn't a hori and he worked at the bus company and they still took him away. If horis are just animals, I've been on farms where there are animals and the sheep have their heads cut off and insides pulled out and no police put anyone in jail. Horis are not like animals at all in that case. Why all along have I been told they were when they weren't, they were men all along. The denim hori was a man and now Winks is going to jail because of me standing at the bend in the stairs and now a man, not an animal, but a man, is dead.

They're still whispering. Heels is saying again to get the hori off the premises, out into a side gutter. It will look as if he and his gang friends blued. She'll help Winks drag him, though she can't stand the thought of touching the hori or his dirty clothes so she'll wear gloves.

I scurry to my bedroom before their door opens. I wait till I hear them leave the apartment, then I follow, not directly to the fire-escape via the kitchen which is the way they're going, they'd see me, but down the staff steps which end at the door with mesh on it that leads onto Tui Street. I unsnib the latch, hop out onto the cold footpath and crash the heavy door closed behind me. There are denim horis and their old cars and motorbikes everywhere. Horis drinking from flagons, the women too, sitting on car bonnets, smoking, or in the gutter or half-leaning half-lying with their backs against the hotel wall for a pillow. They kiss with the women and put their hands into their clothes and the women do the same to them. The air stinks of stale beer, cigarette smoke and petrol fumes, and of denim with BO soaked into it.

I sprint through it all, jumping over the stretched legs and broken glass, shutting out the hoots of those who catch sight of me. One hori tries to grab my ankle but misses and rolls on his side drunk and laughing while the fat woman with him shouts for him to fucking-well leave me alone. She herself lets out a chesty laugh then a wet cough. I run up the hotel's liquor store driveway to the courtyard where the fire-escape slopes overhead to the ground.

Why are Heels and Winks standing there staring at the

concrete at the foot of the fire-escape? Where's the denim hori? Winks makes small chuckling sounds as he speaks. "He was here," he says. "Right here. Exactly this spot."

Heels puts her hands, which are gloved in black evening gloves to the elbow, on her hips as if waiting to do a chore. "He's up and gone. That's what it must be. A lot of fuss and worry for nothing."

What thick skulls those horis have, Winks marvels. Then he says, "What if one of his mates dragged him away dead?"

Heels lets out a snorting sound, almost a laugh. "Who cares? They've done our job for us in that case."

Winks says it would be a weight off his mind to know the hori was actually still alive, but Heels says, "He's off our hands, isn't he? That's the main thing, isn't it?" She peels her evening gloves from her arms.

In the darkness, over there by the beer-crate pen, a long loud sigh. Another sigh, louder, longer. The denim hori staggers into the moon and star light, shaking his cocko dry though lengths of pee still flow out and land on his boots.

"Him!" I shout, pointing and running towards him, elated. I turn to see how relieved Wink must be. Yes, he's smiling and pointing too. But the smile lasts only a second. He orders the hori to "put that thing away." Heels is grimacing. She holds her gloves up to shield her eyes. The denim hori recognises me, grins and makes a stabbing motion as if holding a knife. "Little boss."

"Put that thing away or I'll belt you good and proper this time," yells Winks.

TYPICAL STAFF. A tray of empty glasses in the phone box. Not just on one occasion but all the time recently. They won't own up. Typical. Who else but staff would keep leaving a tray of glasses in such an odd place! Our son? They're accusing our son? They've seen our son coming out of there? What on earth would he be doing with trays in the damned phone box? It's preposterous. "And it's the lowest thing I can imagine," Heels juts. The lowest thing an adult can do—blame a child. An innocent child. *Her* child no less. "It's an insult. I've got a good mind to sack the lot," she sucks and scratches.

Winks asks me one night after dinner, "You don't know anything about trays of glasses in the phone box, do you?"

"No," I reply. I know from previous lies I've told that it's best to look into people's eyes. "Look me in the eye," Heels and Winks say, and teachers and children at school. That way people automatically believe you. I could say, "I swear on my grandmother's grave" which people also take as the truth but I'm not sure yet that there's no afterlife and that my grandmother couldn't haunt me as a punishment.

From now on Heels keeps a close watch on the comings and goings at the phone box. No more trays appear.

*

There is, however, another matter. Mr Atkinson has me standing opposite his dark wood desk. His pipe isn't lit but he's clacking the mouthpiece between his brown teeth and his office pongs of puffed tobacco. "Look me in the eye, young man."

Young man? I've never been called young man before. It sounds threatening, as if he has my measure. Have I reached an age when more will be expected of me, judgments will be harsher, punishments more severe? I'm ten now. Has Mr Atkinson started giving the strap to pakehas like he does the horis? Will he give me the strap now that I'm ten? It's somewhere in this office, the strap. What drawer? That cupboard? He won't give me the strap—he drinks at the Heritage Hotel and Winks serves him. Why is he calling me young man then?

"Have you or have you not been throwing stones at cars?"

I look him in the eye. "No."

"You haven't been?"

"N-n-o." I blink and swallow without meaning to.

Mr Atkinson isn't treating my No as truth. Two boys have been seen just outside the school gates throwing stones at passing cars. A car's windscreen has been broken and one driver, an elderly woman, was very shocked and upset by the impact and was taken to hospital for a lie-down. One of the boys fits my description. The other boy fits Tamoa's description.

It's very difficult to keep looking in his eyes because I *have* been throwing stones at cars. I *have* been trying to hit wind-screens.

"Why would you be involved in that sort of nonsense?" Mr Atkinson asks.

"I d-d-don't know," I answer though I know very well why. I can picture it clearly, throwing the stones, aiming at the sun-smeary windscreens. The bull's-eye. Me running for the cover of the for-climbing-up tree where Tamoa is already hiding barricaded behind the roots that arch out of the ground like rock. When the cars pull over, Minis, Zephyrs, Bedford vans, the driver performs a cursing jig, fists clenched in rage, swearing helpless, defeated by me a child—Tamoa and I mimic the driver to each other.

"You were involved, weren't you?" says Mr Atkinson.

No, I say, looking straight into his eyes. I can't do any more than look him straight in the eye. But I can't keep the straight looking up. I will have to say Yes. "Yes, b-b-but …" What am I to say next? I don't know what I'm going to say.

There's no need to speak. Mr Atkinson leans back in his chair, lights his pipe and does the speaking for me. "I think I know what has happened here," he nods. "Were you roped into this by Tamoa?"

Tamoa. All I have to do is answer Yes and naturally my word will be believed over Tamoa's. "Yes," I answer, looking Mr Atkinson in the eye. Tamoa threw the stones, I lie.

"Why would Tamoa throw stones?" Mr Atkinson asks. I shrug, sullen, silent. Mr Atkinson says he has a theory about why. Tamoa throws stones because he has a chip on his shoul-der: he hates pakehas and since they own most of the cars in Heritage he's at war with them. But you are a pakeha, are you not?, he says. And yet you two have formed a friendship it would seem. There's the weakness in the theory. "You must be an exception to the normal pakeha," Mr Atkinson says with a chuckle of smoke.

I like the idea of being an exception, someone not lumped in with the others. "Y-y-yes, Sir," I say, smiling.

But Mr Atkinson wonders, "Why?" Why would Tamoa want to be friends with me, a pakeha? "Has he ever asked you to take alcohol from your father's hotel?"

"No" (the truth).

"Money from the till?"

"No" (the truth).

"Cigarettes?"

"No" (the truth).

Mr Atkinson frowns, puzzled by my answers. "Well, don't be surprised if he does," he says, sharply. In the meantime he'll have to put us two being pals down to opposites attracting. Neither of us makes friends easily. But I mustn't let a desire for friends lead me to make poor choices in life. There's nothing wrong with being curious about those who are different from you, and there are some fine Maoris about, but beware of the wrong sort.

His gentle, lowered voice soothes me. His sweet, leaf-smoke smell soothes me. He stands up from his chair and walks over to place his hand on my shoulder, breathing a pipe cloud onto my head, the embodiment for me now of kindness, wisdom, authority, mercy. I am in awe of him. I love him. I'm ashamed he had to explain my errors to me. I should have realised them myself. I should never have made those errors in the first place. Does he think less of me? What can I do to make him stop thinking less of me? "Tamoa m-m-made me th-h-throw the st-t-ones," I lie and stare up into Mr Atkinson's face desperate for a sign of redemption.

His hairy brown eyes slope down and pucker. "He did?"

"He said he'd b-b-beat me up if I d-d-didn't d-d-do it."

Mr Atkinson lets out a long, smoky sigh. He pats my shoulder, nods and smiles, satisfied.

I hurry through his waiting room back to class, passing Tamoa. I keep my head bowed, avoiding Tamoa's face. I could turn around and admit my lie. Turn around now! I can bear the strap, the shame. No, I can't. I don't want to bear them. Besides, it's too late. Mr Atkinson will have taken the strap from its special drawer. There! I can hear it snap once, twice, another time, another. Tamoa will wear the red welts like a badge of honour. Surely he will. Forget Tamoa, he's not a fine Maori.

But I can't forget Tamoa. Heels would forget him, Winks would too. "Don't waste your time worrying about the likes of him," they'd say. I'm their son. I should think as they think. Be as they would be. I should have faith in their ways. Now there is a double betrayal, of Tamoa and of Heels and Winks.

The Tamoa betrayal is the one that needs my immediate attention because he's waiting for me when school finishes. At first he's silent, sulky, eyes puffy from what can only be an afternoon's crying. As I attempt to cut across the lawn away from him he follows. When I go the other way through the front gate he follows. Across the traffic lights and over the rail-line he follows. I notice he limps slightly and tugs at his shorts as if to relieve a discomfort. Suddenly he begins a haka, screaming out hori words I don't understand from deep in himself so that his voice rasps. He rushes up to me to unleash the chant, the slapping of his chest, shivering hands and tongue poking in-out-in-out, directly in my face. His eye corners and nose glisten with tears and snot. I flinch expecting him to throw me to the ground and hit me. If he does I'm going to let him do it and not resist or fight back. I'm terrified of being hurt but Tamoa seems to have a right to hurt me in this case and I'll have to take my punishment. His revenge will make me clean again.

No, I will fight. I brace myself ready to punch and scratch and bite with everything I'm worth. Yet all he does is rant his haka and let me walk by without laying a finger on me. It's not until I'm well up the street that he speaks English. "When I'm Prime Minister I'll cut your fucking throat *e hoa*," he calls out. I walk on. He calls louder. "I asked what onions are *e hoa*. When a whole lot of horis stick their cockos in a girl. My cousin says they piss on them too and pour petrol on them if they don't like them and flick matches, *e hoa*. I'm getting my cousin to do that to your mother. The Mongrel Mob are coming to onion your mother."

Tamoa isn't at school the next day or the next day. I want to plead with him, give him cigarettes and a bottle of beer I've stolen from the Private Bar and stashed in the for-climbing-up tree. I want to be friends again and have him promise the Mongrel Mob will never onion Heels. But Mrs Quigley says, "I'm afraid he's been wagging. Don't you bother your head about that sorry case."

I must warn Heels. The Mongrel Mob's coming to onion her. But that would mean revealing why they're coming, that I was the real stone-thrower. I must protect her. But I can't protect her all day, when I'm at school. Some job I did protecting the stairs from *one* denim hori, let alone a whole gang.

Now is my chance to speak up. Heels and Winks are standing at the foot of my bed. It's one of my growth-spurt days, almost noon. I lie beneath the blankets, sweaty, an ache in my head, ears crackling when I swallow. They want to have a word. It can't be about the phone box—I've learned my lesson and always return my tray of dregs to the Private Bar sink however woozy I might be. It must be the cigarettes and bottle of beer I stole for Tamoa. There is an especially severe clench to Winks' face. His dark, deep-set eyes have narrowed to slits. Heels' jaw is jutting, she's building up to her sucking and scratching stage. It's not a good time to speak up, I sense. I sit hugging the blankets over my knees.

"You never told us you fell off your bike," says Winks. I'm relieved. Yes, I did fall off my bike on the way to elocution at Mrs Daley's. My cardboard case that carries my recital poems toppled from its perch between the handlebars and somehow lodged in the front wheel spokes. This jammed the bike and flipped me through the air onto the road. No harm done. The spokes were a bit bent but I straightened them.

"We understand you were very upset," Winks continues. Yes, I suppose I was upset. I got a shock, I tell him. Just a shock that's all.

"*That's all*, he says," snarls Heels.

"I'll handle this," snaps Winks, cutting her off. He glares at me. "Upset enough that when a perfectly decent woman, a Mrs ..."

"Pritchard," prompts Heels.

"Pritchard offers to help you to your feet and dust you off, you ..." His temper is blazing in his face. "You shout at her to f ..."

Heels holds up her hand to prevent him uttering the word. Winks' cheeks swell with holding his breath until he can think of an alternative word.

"To … to … intercourse off."

It's true. Sprawled on the road in front of a few old ladies, embarrassed, I said it. I think about calling the old woman a liar. If this Mrs Pritchard was a hori I might get away with it, but Heels and Winks wouldn't be so angry in the first place if she was hori. Instead I sputter that it was a spur-of-the-moment mistake and I'll never do it again. Heels sucks and scratches that I most certainly *won't* do it again. For half an hour she's been on the phone to Mrs Pritchard apologising for my disgusting behaviour, behaviour that I never learned from her, a lack of manners, a foul mouth and lack of common courtesy. When she thinks of the sacrifices she and Winks have made for me, slaving their guts out in a hotel with hori animals just to give me a future, only to be rewarded like this, to be let down and disappointed like this.

She nods to Winks and he removes his belt, drawing it from his trouser hoops like a bendy sword the way he's done in the past. But this time there's none of his theatrical tap-tapping of the belt on his open hand as a warning. He mutters, "Jesus bloody Christ, I'll teach you a thing or two." His face quakes with temper like I've only seen it do when he and Charlie Carmichael clip the winter coats from his horses and they won't stand still in their stall so he flogs them with the clipper cord till they snort and pant in terrified submission.

He claws up a fistful of blankets and flings them from me. He orders me to "roll over, roll over" and when I won't do as he says he hooks his fingers in my pyjama-pant elastics and lifts and spins me onto my stomach, pulls the elastic down at the same time to expose my buttocks. The elastic breaks. My pyjama pants rip like paper.

I flick myself off the bed and shimmy under it for protection. The springs sag and squeak from Winks diving across to try and tackle me. Now he's on his knees groping for a hold of me in the dusty narrowness. I shuffle away from his grasp into the open field of the room where Heels sucks and scratches for me to be still and take the medicine that's coming to me. She snatches at my arms but I wriggle free, crying, crying how sorry I am and I'll never swear again. Sorry's not going to help me now, Heels juts, bear-hugging me onto the bed. I butt her breasts with the back of my head, kick backwards into her shins. I sink my teeth into her forearm. She squeals, releases her grip and bursts into tears, disowning and cursing me for fighting back. "He's bitten me. Your son has bitten me," she shows Winks. This sends him into a frenzy with the belt. He whips my arse and legs. He forces my face into the sheets to stop me reaching around and catching the belt mid-air. I almost jerk it away from him but all this does is work the buckle loose from inside his hand. When he starts whipping again it's the buckle that makes contact with a rhythmic slap-clink. A sting-burn-numbness ricochets into the bottom of my spine and down to my big toes. I slide my head sideways. My eye meets Winks' eye. His arm freezes like a man about to throw a ball. He's heaving to catch his breath. Sweat-drops hang from his nose and top lip. His eyes water suddenly and his chin twitches. He bares his teeth and brings his arm down once, twice, three, four, five times, not hitting me, but letting off blows into the mattress beside me.

He stands with his legs wide apart, heaving and threading his belt into place. He doesn't look at me. He inspects Heels' bite-wound, wets it with spit-kisses.

"To think I nearly died having him," sobs Heels. She means the operation she had to have me born properly.

I wish she *had* died. What a terrible thing to think. I think it again and then say it in my mind to know if I mean it. Yes I do mean it. I enjoy thinking it. There's no shock or guilt in thinking it and meaning it. If anything there's excitement. I mumble it into the sheets. "I wish you had died." I repeat it to the sheets and say, "The Mongrel Mob are coming and I don't care."

Heels and Winks stare at me, probably thinking I'm apologising.

Something freeing is happening. Here I lie, no tears, no pain. Where's pain? Where's fear? I've passed through these into a state of sleepy peace. The sting-burn-numb sensation has contracted to the base of my spine. It has now become a pleasant tickle deep inside me, an itchy pins and needles at the tips of my fingers. I don't move a muscle, I can't move a muscle. My legs won't shift. Only my mind works, I conjure a force field around me, one able to push Heels from me, a weightless push and drift of her away from my skin, my heart, my being. What about Winks? Is he going to be pushed away too? Not yet. Not quite. I'm still pushing Heels away. But his turn is coming. It's close.

She's gone. Now it's Winks' turn. I push. He's up there tightening his belt around his waist. He's touching Heels' sore arm, leading her out of the room. The door's closing. There they go. They're gone.

*

A glass of milk and two shortbreads, my favourite. She sets them down on the bedside table. She calls me *darling*. She wants to make up, to get back into each other's good books as she would say. She expects it to happen just like that. She probably thinks it has already happened by some natural process. Her arm sports a brown strip of plaster. I've been alone in my room for an hour on my bed. Is that meant to be my strip of plaster? "Sit up and have your shortbreads," she urges.

It's Winks' turn. He sits on the bed and tousles my hair. I flinch and shrink from the sudden lift of his hand, its warm weight, though I feel myself returning his smiling—I can't help doing it. He says it gave him no pleasure taking the belt to my hide but bad habits have to be knocked out of us. He even winks and says he's impressed by the way I fought back. I'm growing up, showing some gumption. Goodness gracious how strong I'm getting. I return his smile again, and Heels' smile as well, proud of the compliments.

I crave the milk and shortbreads but won't allow myself to touch them, won't allow those two hovering over me to have the pleasure of my pleasure in eating and drinking. Winks places his hand gently on my rump. I sniff sharply from the pain. "Sore?" he asks, smiling and nodding so that I understand that he knows what it's like to be sore.

"No," I lie, enjoying contradicting him.

"Not sore?" He's doubting me.

"N-n-no." How dare he doubt me.

He pats my bum, testing me. I disguise the blood-throb of pain with a cough. "Whatever you say," he grins.

I want to dig my fingernails into his arms and tear away skin for his grinning. "I can't f-f-feel anything f-f-from here (meaning my hips) d-d-down to th-th-there (meaning my toes)." How shall I keep up this lie? I have to imitate what it was like straight after the belting, that feeling of no feeling, dead legs. Winks and his sudden grinless look, serious, concerned, are worth the risk.

"Nothing at all? No feeling?" he asks. Heels is concerned now. The brown pencil-lines she wears for eyebrows fidget as she blinks. Winks eases the blankets from my naked body. I play paralysed as he pokes and prods at my skinny legs and feet, my ribby stomach, trying for a response. "No feeling?"

I shake my head. No feeling. He and Heels take careful hold of my hips and turn me onto my side. This will be the hard part. They're going to start fingering those welts, the ones that look like I've been sitting in a cane chair. I'm going to have to withstand the hurting. I'll recite my times tables to keep a blank face, think of all the best exotic, adventure-sounding names of racehorses I've seen in the newspaper, and shuffle the words into poems the way I like doing. "Dashing Star, Ragtag Kingdom, Desert Honour, Tang, Storm Mouth," equals:

The desert honours the ragtag kingdom
With a dashing star and the storm mouth's tang

Their fingers feel between the marks on my thighs, arse-cheeks, back. They're being so careful with their touch they almost tickle. I'm enjoying this tenderness. Their fingertips stroke and soothe me. I must harden myself against their affection, against them. Look at their faces, they work so hard to maintain beautiful faces—Winks with his razor and Old Spice aftershave; Heels with her bottles and tubs of scent, lipstick, powder and Ponds. They have lines in their faces deep as the lines in the hand's palm, saggy, blotchy skin. Heels often admires my skin, "so smooth and without a single solitary blemish. You're so lucky," she says. "What a lucky boy to have such lovely skin and have been born in Sydney. You have landed on your feet."

These ways, skin and Sydney, are not the only ways I've become aware of being superior to her, to them both. Heels' is a butcher's daughter. I am once removed from a butcher as a relation, from those blood-greasy hands they have, a finger missing, an apron wiped with gore. Heels watches television and doesn't ever read. For me it's the other way round—no TV but books, books, books. She says she doesn't need to improve herself, she's improved enough, but I noticed that Jane Austen's *Persuasion* recently appeared beside her bed. I teased her about it but she set me straight. She said, "It's really just there for show, for when people are coming through to value the place for buying."

Heels is good at maths and counts coins from her desk two at a time as if dusting fast. I'm hopeless at maths. That, as far as I can tell, is her only victory over me. Winks reads books, thrillers and Westerns, and watches TV but he can't draw like I can. He can't spell a word like *philosophical*. He's the son of a barber. I'm glad Winks' life stands between mine and a man who would have been covered in other people's hair.

They don't know it but I've found them out. Horis are no more likely to be drunks than pakehas. What about Charlie Carmichael who drinks till he dribbles and slurs when he talks? Even if horis were, who is it that's giving them the liquor in the first place? These two right here standing over me. When the phone rings after nine at night—"Horis again, Dad?"—it's not always horis. What about when the card schools start fighting over cheating? They roll up their sleeves and mark out a boxing ring with chairs but the blood spilled is blood nonetheless no matter how they pretend to fight like proper gentlemen.

And there's my own grandfather—Winks' dad, the barber. He was a no-hoper who drank himself to death. I've heard it from Heels' own lips. He hit my grandmother till she was black and blue and nobody ever said he was a hori.

What about me, taking trays into the phone box? Next they'll be calling me a hori. Maybe I am. Maybe we're secretly horis and hating them so no one will catch on that there's brown in us. We probably have our own version of onions.

Next time I meet a male adult hori I will shake his hand and address him as Sir as if he was one of us. I will address the men as Sir and the women as Mrs Whatever or Miss Whatever. I imagine myself saying it. It isn't that easy to think of a hori as a Sir or Mrs or Miss. Especially the denim horis. Perhaps I can't do it after all. It would be easier to go back to the way things were taught to me. I wish I'd never found Heels and Winks out. If only the next time I met a hori I could imagine spitting in his eye as normal.

What are they saying over there about the doctor? Heels wants to fetch Dr Murchison. They've moved away from the bed for a hush-talk. "Oh, let him ask about the bruises," she's saying. "Dr Murchison will understand. He's from the old school."

Dr Murchison. He won't be fooled by my legs not working. He'll have all sorts of tests and stethoscopes to check for feeling and expose my lie. I might never be able to lie again. And what a hiding I'll get. "I can feel something," I say in pretend pain. I shift my legs beneath the blankets and let out a groan of effort. Heels quick-steps to the bed. Winks strides to the opposite side and lifts the blankets. They sigh and make a phewing-whistling sound. "Darling," she says kissing my forehead. Winks rubs the crown of my hair and says "That's my boy. Move some more."

I raise and bend my legs, groan and wince, spurred on by the sighs and *that's my boy* clucking. I'm lifted very tenderly to a sitting position, Winks' hand for a chair-back. I relax into his hand, reassured, comforted, warmed. A shortbread and glass of milk are lifted to my lips. I nibble and sip and remind myself that I'm still acting, I'm not giving in to any love.

To prove it, I'm going to run away. Tonight. I'm almost eleven, it's time I stood on my own two feet. Winks left home at eleven—those timber yards and gravel pits and one roast potato for dinner Heels goes on about. It must be such a frightening thing and a lonely thing to do. But it seems to be admired in him, all part of having lived a life where you've worked hard and have the right to boast about it and criticise others for not having done the same.

It is expected of me, leaving home, it's obvious to me. For other boys the time will eventually arrive but for me the time is now. Heels and Winks have successfully weaned me. Is that what has happened? As horses are weaned I have been weaned: first by turning me against horis, then Heritage, and now by turning me against *them*. I'm ready to go, to step out into the world. I suppose there's no to-do or ceremony about it. No teary goodbye or the like. Winks never spoke of ceremonies or a great to-do or teary goodbye for him. I just pack my bag and slip out, that's probably the way I'm expected to go.

Sydney's a warm place. A cardigan, two shirts, some singlets, underwear, socks. Never that goat coat. Toothbrush. Toothpaste. The shoes I'm already wearing. It won't all fit into my school satchel so I'll put on my pants, the ones Heels calls my casual slacks, and wear my good pants, the ones for going out, under them, the ones Heels calls special. I'll wear my cardigan under my windcheater. One shirt. One singlet. A pair of socks. One lot of underwear. No toothbrush or Macleans. I roll them up tight and stuff them in. An apple. Two apples to tide me over. How will I pay for food and for tickets? Someone will pay. Someone always pays. *Has* paid up till now. But now it will be different.

There's that donation money for the Celtic softball club in the beer mug on the Private Bar bar. It's not going to be enough and it's all in coins, heavy coins. The till money is hidden in those calico bags under Winks' bedside for morning banking. Surely it's not stealing, not in my case, my being his son. It's more like initiative. What if it is stealing? Just a few notes out of those calico bags isn't stealing. Some cigarette packs for trading with someone for something, for food. A few bottles of beer for trading or drinking? I can't cart bottles of beers around. I'll take a couple or three notes from the calico bag, and the softball club change no matter how heavy. A message to say goodbye, in my best handwriting: *I'm leaving. Thank you for everything. Goodbye.* I don't put *Love* at the end of the message as a punishment for the beating and being made to wear the goat coat to the factory.

*

Why don't the trains stop? Every night they clitter-clatter past my bedroom window. They clitter-clatter past on the hour or thereabouts when the clock dongs ten, twelve, one, waking me pleasantly, but they're not stopping. I stand on the platform, the only person, waving, shouting at the blur of steel boxes and tree-trunks but the blur shouts back an icy wind and then the platform goes quiet and the air settles on me with all the wet chill of a frost. Am I standing in the wrong place? No. This is Heritage Station, a stone's throw from the hotel, the centre of town. This is the place where trains stop.

They blur and shout past, blur and shout. I can't keep awake any more. But I can't quite fall asleep because of the awful cold. I sit on a slat bench, I lie on it but it's just a damp bed of cold. I curl up in the doorway, pull up my legs. My eyelids keep closing, so heavy, they're so heavy.

"Wee fella. Up you go, wee fella." The Senior Sergeant. His pyjama collars poke out from his scratchy-wool jumper. His breath is sleep-smelling breath, the way breath gets in the mornings.

The hotel corridor. My eyelids open and close on Heels. She is kneeling, chin twitching with tearfulness. She is sucking and jutting, rifling through my satchel, the cigarette packs it contained stacked at her feet. The higher the stack grows—three storeys high—the louder she sucks the air.

"Boys will be boys," the Senior Sergeant says and thanks Winks for the crate of beer at his feet. Winks is holding me. He tosses me tighter into his chest for a better grip. His chest is warming me.

*

Weaning? What's all this nonsense about weaning?, Heels wants to know. It is morning. She's jutting and scratching, saying that no one could be so stupid as to expect her to believe such tripe. You're not a half-wit, are you? You're supposed to be a clever boy for all your stutter speech. Too clever for your own good. Your weaning story is just that—a story, a cock and bull story, a load of hooey. They have never turned you against others, she says—horis or otherwise. They, as responsible parents, have simply told you the facts as they see them. Don't try and make your own mother and father feel guilty for opening your eyes to the world. And never ever accuse them of driving you away—this so-called weaning business. As for your stealing, you are a little thief, young man, someone who stole cigarettes and then got it into his head that he should run away from home which is a kick in the teeth for her and a kick in the teeth for your father. No one could know what pain *is* till they are a mother who nearly died having their child and then are kicked in the teeth by that child running away from home. What shall they do!

Perhaps a word with Dr Murchison is called for, merely to enquire about seeing someone, one of those psychiatrist types, Winks suggests. *Never*, Heels flares. Never, never, never. "I'd die from embarrassment. No son of mine needs a psychiatrist," she says. No use in thrashing you, though she'd like to see it. What good has it done? They've decided to do the following: you will go to work after school with old Hugh McPherson washing bottles in the liquor store. You will learn some responsibility. You will learn to pull your weight. You want to make your own way in the world? Start at the bottom and work your way up. Start by washing bottles and flagons with Hugh McPherson. Now, give your mother a hug and say how sorry you are. A bit more convincing please. Now a kiss. A bit more meaningful please. That's better. Eat your breakfast.

*

Start at the bottom and work my way up. I have no intention of starting at the bottom. I'm better than that. I have been given every advantage in life and have been given that advantage so that I would not have to start at the bottom like Heels and Winks. They themselves have always made that clear. Washing beer bottles and flagons for refilling—that's old Hugh's job. That's all he's good for. How can *he* be in charge of *me*?

"Don't go easy on the boy," Winks orders Hugh, old Hugh with his gargling Scottish voice and purple scribble of veins on his nose and cheeks. He's *staff*. He's so bald I can see the thin brown baby-hairs sprouting on his shiny crown. Yet he's telling me what to do, this old man with a solitary black strand of hair swept over his head and hooked over his ear and around his earlobe. He sweats and loses his breath just from saying hello to customers coming to the counter past the buzzing robotic eye.

I sit on a crate in front of the bottle-washing contraption in the backroom. The air reeks of washed-out beer. Hugh instructs me to push a beer bottle onto each brush claw then to push this little button here and set the water awhisk. The glass is washed, rinsed, dried with a blow of hot air. When this red light here lights up, pull the bottles from the claws and place them upside down in this rack for refilling with beer.

At first Hugh resents my presence. "Are they saying an eleven-year-old can do my job?" he grumbles. Yet clearly he enjoys bossing me. "Well don't just sit there like the landed fucking gentry, get to work," he orders because I work slowly, sulkily, in protest. After attaching each bottle to the contraption I pause, day-dream. I read the labels on cartons and crates stacked halfway to the ceiling and blend them with racehorse names from the newspaper to make more poems: *Storm draught dashes the ragtag walker and the white horse that was Napoleon's honour.*

"For Christ's sake speed up lad. You'll get me into fucking trouble with your go-slow," complains Hugh.

This man I've barely said a word to, who is neither my father nor a teacher nor a relative, is ordering me about. *Ordering*. He takes his red tartan thermos and stands at the counter pouring himself a lidful.

I speed up my work as if in a race to fill the drying rack the fastest it has ever been filled. It will show Winks what a slouch shuffle-footed Hugh is as a washer and how cheerfully and efficiently I go about my job so that it's hardly a punishment at all and therefore there's no point in keeping me at it.

"Slow down," demands Hugh. "Do me out of a fucking job, would you?" But I don't slow down. "Slow down," he demands again. "Play the game lad." I don't slow down. "Laddie, laddie, play the game. Play the game, lad. Come on, take a break. Take a break. Come have some coffee."

I've never tasted coffee. Hugh sits down on an upturned crate and pours splashes of coffee into his thermos cup-cap. The liquid smells and tastes sourly of liquorice yet has been heavily sweetened. My lips are sticky with sugar. After the first few bitter sips the flavour becomes more palatable.

"Bet that fucking well slows you down," Hugh sniggers with his jiggling belly. I take longer sips. Heat rises in my face not unlike the feeling I get from the trays in the phone box. I say as much to Hugh. "I f-f-feel like I d-do when I d-d-rink the d-d-dregs in the ph-phone box."

Hugh stops sniggering and swigging directly from his

thermos. "So it was *you* after all, you little cunt. Folks nearly got fired over that." His mouth purses into a grin. "Well there's good Scotch whisky in that coffee lad, not fucken dregs. Good Scotch whisky."

I try to stand but my legs won't let me. Hugh's voice seems very distant and sometimes heard only in my left ear. Sometimes only in my right. "That's slowed you down, hasn't it lad? Ay, you sit there quietly and be at peace with the fucking world."

I hear buzzing—the robotic eye is buzzing. Hugh hobbles off in its direction. I must go up the stairs to bed. Are these my stairs? This ladder is very like my stairs. Up I go to bed. This is a landing with crates and cartons, it's not my bedroom. Back down the ladder. Forget the ladder. I can make it to the ground in one stride. I step out. The ground is lifting up. Dark.

Winks is slapping my face with his fingertips. I've woken to his crying and slapping and laughing that I'm not dead, that I've fallen all this way and barely have a mark on me. He is feeling my arms and legs again for breaks. None, he says. There seems to be no blood on my head, just a blue bump in my hairline.

He bends forward to embrace me. Hesitates. Smells my breath. "He's drunk. He bloody stinks of the stuff. He's drunk," he says, muttering at first then almost yelling.

"There's your mystery of the phone box solved," Hugh is desperate to explain. "Little bugger stole my flu toddy right from under my nose."

AUSTRALIA IS AN ENGLAND OF New Zealand. If you sell a hotel for $400,000 and you are a pakeha, naturally you will want to leave Heritage. You will want to live somewhere else, want to graduate to a place that is bigger, more serious in the world scheme of things. A city, a great city. Is Sydney a great city? From Heritage it seems to be. Other people leave for England—the *real* England. Everybody leaves at some time, though *they* leave temporarily, a year or two of what is called O.E.—overseas experience—in the land where their grandparents or great-grandparents were born, rickety paupers, housemaids, labourers, miners, dockers, those we call ancestors.

Ancestors. What do *our* kind, Heels, Winks and me, care about ancestors. Ancestors is hori talk. Only horis and snobs who want to trace themselves back to the Earl of somewhere or other care about ancestors. "What did ancestors ever do for us?" is our opinion of ancestors.

Australia is *our* England. Ancestors left England for a better life, and we are going to Sydney where I myself was born. I am my own ancestor.

"Someone's leaving for greener pastures," Mrs Quigley announces on my last day at school. She asks me to stand up in class and explain where, when and why we are going. She hasn't warned me she would do this and surely she knows I hate standing up in front of people.

"Up. Up," she motions with her fingers as if stroking something. "Up. Up."

I get to my feet, hands clasped in front of me, trying to close myself off. Mrs Quigley repeats the question. "Now, where are you departing our fair shores for, and when and why?"

After the fall from the landing a remarkable thing happened. When I sobered up from the bang on the head and the fog of the drink and said my first sentence—"Sorry. I'm sorry."—the words came out of my mouth clear, with no false starts. The two sorrys had one S each, not three or four. No stutter. My stuttering disappeared. It's cured. Dr Murchison has never heard the like. The only trace is a vague, whistly lisp. I've never known such happiness. It's probably not even happiness but a feeling far greater. I can be happy eating the crisp rind from bacon or on Sundays when the hotel is closed and the bars and rooms are silent and empty and mine all to myself. But this is a feeling that swells inside me with such pressure it takes my breath away, it makes me want to laugh though nothing funny has happened, and cry as if suffering from sheer pleasure.

On the day my stuttering died I vowed to speak as often and as loud as possible all those once feared words with the Fs and Ths, Ss and Ps. I rattled off "feather, father, system, slice of pickled pepper" to Heels and Winks, running on the spot with excitement. Heels hugged me so tight into her bosom my new, pure speech was momentarily muffled and I strained impatiently to get away. And Winks' eyes—I'm sure they were wet. He turned his face from me and gripped the back of a chair. His shoulders quaked. I skipped around my bedroom saying, "fans and farmers thick as thieves in sport and pirates" as Heels and Winks settled into bickering.

Her: "We all have me to thank for this. If I hadn't insisted on elocution lessons he'd still be jabbering."

Him: "It was his fall."

"I'm not interested in any fall thank you very much. *Elocution lessons*."

"He's been having those lessons for a bloody year."

"And now they've finally paid dividends."

"He was drunk from stealing from Hugh's flask and fell off the landing, love."

"I don't want to talk about that."

"And it was him in the bloody phone box."

"I can't bear it. The embarrassment. It's all around town. As far as I'm concerned none of it ever happened. My son no longer stutters because of elocution lessons."

Her eyes had narrowed as if fighting back tears. No tears came. She buried her fingernails deep into her stiff hair-do and scratched it in time with her heavy breathing. The scratching made a static sound come crackling out of her scalp. She spoke to Winks through clenched teeth. "If you're so clever then, then, then … what else has the bang on the head cured? Has it cured his being ungrateful? Has it cured his foul-mouthed manners? Or just singled out his stuttering? How nice for him."

Winks: "Leave it out, love."

"When have you heard him ever thank me? Thank me

for elocution lessons, for the lovely clothes, for slaving my guts out in this God-forsaken place? I've done everything for him."

"This is a big moment for him. Let's not spoil it."

"This miraculous bang on the head, has it cured him from writing left-handed? Has it?"

I skipped in circles, chanted my Ss and Ps. She grabbed my left hand—"Stop that ridiculous dancing. Stop it and shut up!"—and pinched the string tied to my index finger and held up my hand by this thread. "Has it cured this? Has it? Has it?"

She pointed me to the chair at my corner desk by the window. "Sit. Sit. Pen. Get a pen." She pushed me aside, fingered out a slip of paper from the desk pigeonhole and snapped it down in front of me. I held a pen in my hand waiting for instructions. "See?" she hissed to Winks. She gripped my hand, my left hand which held the pen, and shook it. "He still picks up the pen with his left hand. He hasn't been broken of it." She snatched the pen out of my hand so fiercely that saliva bubbled in front of her bared teeth and I flinched expecting a blow. She prised the pen into the fingers of my right hand. "Open your paw. Open your paw." She took a step backwards. "Now write. Go on. Write."

"Write what?" I said.

"Don't you talk back to me. Do as I say and write."

"But I don't know what to write."

"If you don't write something right this moment you'll never write a damned thing again, so help me."

Winks groans, a long groan of frustration, "Just write your bloody name: 'Hello, my name is,' just to make her happy."

My hand looped and dragged the pen as best it could until a spindly, unreadable scrawl was completed.

"Exactly what I thought," Heels said victoriously. "This miraculous bang on the head doesn't extend to handwriting. What *does* extend to handwriting is telling him over and over again until it finally sinks into his thick skull that he must never write with the hand with the string on it. And practising over and over to write with his right hand will eventually work. Just like, as far as I'm concerned, and I won't be contradicted, the elocution lessons have fixed his stutter. In fact I want it known throughout Heritage that I'll be paying Mrs Daley a fifty-dollar bonus for her wonderful efforts."

*

Now that I'm standing before the class, all those eyes watching, I wish I could stutter again. Mrs Quigley would never have got me to stand if I stuttered.

"What country are you headed for?" she persists.

"Aust-st-st-stralia." Is this tempting fate? Will pretending to stutter bring the stuttering back forever? I quickly sit down. "Australia. Australia," I say under my breath, testing each syllable in my mouth. "Australia. Australia."

Mrs Quigley knows I was pretending. Look at her eyebrow cocked into an upside-down U. Those ripples of skin the same shape above it. My classmates snigger that they know I'm pretending.

"Up. Up. We haven't finished with you yet, have we children? Tell us why you are headed for Australia."

"Because he's a drunk," someone shouts—a girl, maybe Bronwyn. Maybe Sandra. The children, all of them, giggle and shout, "In a phone box. Drunk in a phone box."

Mrs Quigley shushes them. "Alcohol and its harmful effects are no laughing matter. I will not have jokes of that nature in my classroom."

"He was so drunk he fell and it fixed his stoppage, Mrs."

"It was elocution lessons," I counter, a feeble protest against the class's glee.

"I said shsh," Mrs Quigley says and claps her hands until the noise ceases. "I was hoping to have an intelligent few minutes but clearly that is beyond you. Our newpaper has deemed the sale of the Heritage Hotel worthy of inclusion in its pages." She picks up a copy of the *Chronicle* from her desk and shakes it inside out to the relevant page. "I would have hoped that this article might prompt among us a discussion on what, if anything, the sale might mean for our town. I read here in the paper that the hotel will be pulled down and replaced by a department store. That will be a big change for Tui Street, I'm sure. Quite a boon perhaps. But such a discussion is of no interest to this class it seems."

"He's rich," someone calls out: Peter, the accountant's son.

Mrs Quigley claps her hands. "Enough. Enough. Money does not equal happiness, children."

Arms go up, repeatedly bending and stiffening to be noticed. "Mrs Quigley, Mrs Quigley," the class pleads. Mrs Quigley orders them to be quiet and to keep their hands in their laps, but they ignore her and blather three or four at a time desperate for a say about money, which they refer to as my money—"his $400,000"—as if it represents all the money in the world.

"My mother says what a lot of mouths that would feed. She says what a lot of shoes for little feet."

"Mine wants to know how such a lot of money could come out of Heritage."

"My dad reckons it shouldn't be allowed to leave town. It should be put back into the town because it comes from here."

"My dad says if it's grog money it's dirty money."

"Your dad's a Salvo."

Mrs Quigley stomps her feet. "I don't think we're old enough to discuss these matters properly. We shall do our times tables, please. I said we'll do our times tables, please." She gives an exaggerated nod of the head, a signal for me to resume my seat, which I do though immediately I regret it because the class's laughing presses down on me. I should have stayed on my feet. I should say—Heels would say it— that they aren't worth worrying about, these low-grade types with their sniggering. She would stand up and say right this minute that it was elocution lessons that cured my stuttering. She would say it over and over until they shut their mouths and either believed her or she was forced to tell them how disgraceful and insulting it is that they don't believe her. If they don't want to believe what she's telling them, that's their problem, even if what she's telling them is a lie, because there's no such thing as a lie if you believe the lie is truth the way Heels has the trick of doing. Elocution lessons cure stuttering if you believe it's true and state it definitely enough like she does.

Them with their $400,000-talk—they're just jealous. Their fathers aren't worth a cent. They're nobodies in a no-hoper town like Heritage. It's not possible to feel shame among types like these. "Your name's mud," someone yells. But I forgive them because I couldn't expect better from the likes of these. I smile at them, offer a snort of a laugh. I will never see these people again after this day. I want them to imagine that they and their opinions and ridicule mean nothing to me and never could do.

AUSTRALIA IS WHERE SYDNEY turns off into Randwick and Randwick turns off into Dutruc Street and the khaki brick flats where a concrete path turns into a stairwell through glass swing doors, up three flights of steps to a cramped lounge with a spongy fake leopard-skin table-like square called a pouf in the centre of the room.

Why is this flat being called a flat when it's in Sydney? Flats are supposed to be called apartments here like in Paris and America because they're so much nicer than flats which is a depressing and dowdy name for a place to live. Sydney is not what I expected at all. Surely $400,000 would buy a palace! Heels says the $400,000 is no longer worth $400,000. Even if it was, $400,000 would not buy a palace in Sydney. And what's the point of a palace anyway if after buying it you don't have anything left over to put food on the table? We are renting this flat to tide us over until a suitable business can be found to purchase and *then* we will buy an apartment, a proper apartment.

She's cleaning the stove, rubber gloves streaming with the wet black grime she scours with steel wool. When that's finished, the bathroom tiles get the same treatment till the bleach fumes cause her eyes to run.

"If we're renting, aren't we one of those who don't care? Can't we relax?" I ask.

"You never know who was here before us," she pants, then pats her hair-do in place with her wrist, then scrubs and pants.

Now she's doing subtraction from the original $400,000 out loud, mumbling something about a mortgage on the Heritage Hotel, something else about bringing a dollar from New Zealand to here and only getting 80 cents. She gripes about this to the floor, shoving the steel wool along the bath as if digging now rather than scrubbing.

"What's a mortgage?" I ask.

Heels gives an extra shove across the bath at the very mention of the word. "A mortgage is a debt that the bank has over you."

"How can they do that?"

"Because we ask them to," she says impatiently. "And please don't start harping on with 'Why? Why?' There's a million things like mortgages in life."

"Like what?"

"Like tax. There's tax to be paid when you sell a business."

"Why?"

"The government wants to punish you for making something of yourself. You'll find out when you grow up and have businesses of your own."

"What else?"

"Millions of things."

The good news is that the government in Australia is a hopeless Labor government and because of that interest rates are going up, up, up on the money we've got in the bank. That's what happens with Labor governments, she exhales heavily, giving another wrist-pat to her hair. Labor governments don't like our sort of people; get up and go sort of people. An interest rate is like a thank-you that banks pay you for letting them use your money. They thank you more when there's a bad government. "Think of a piece of paper where there's a right-hand column and a left-hand column. The thank-you goes in the left-hand column because that's where the good news goes. The bad news goes in the right-hand column."

In the good news column we can put $10,000 for selling the Mercedes to Sir Thomas Goodes' family. But we need to buy a new car now that we're in Australia. Something that's not too much of a comedown from a Mercedes. That will have to go in the bad news column. The bad news column is just a little too full for Heels' liking. For that she blames Winks.

"Why?"

"Because he's gone off and done a ridiculous thing." She's beginning to jut and scratch the air. She's talking to me but intending the words for Winks because of the way she cranes her neck and raises her voice to aim it out the door.

"What has he done?" I ask.

"Before we left New Zealand he bought himself a yearling at the horse sales in Wellington. Not just any yearling, mind you. A $15,000 thing."

"Why did he do that?"

"You go ask *him*. I've got my theories. It's simply so he can big-note himself in Sydney with an expensive horse if you ask me."

I do go and ask him. He has spread newspaper on the kitchen table for nuggeting his good shoes. His race-day shoes. "Why did you buy an expensive horse?"

He waves me away with a shoe on his hand like a boxing glove. "Don't *you* start," he says with complaining in his voice. "This colt's by Pakistan out of a Star Kingdom mare. A champion in the making. I can feel it in my water."

Heels yells from the bathroom, "Feel it in your water? Who ever heard of such hooey! Besides the bloody thing won't be a colt much longer. I don't hear you mentioning that he's more interested in mounting fillies than racing in races. He's got to be gelded. So there's vet fees to go in the bad news column. Along with the plane fare to fly the thing to Sydney, and training fees."

Winks is polishing his shoe so fiercely his hair that is usually Brylcreemed perfectly in place is falling loose over his forehead.

Heels keeps adding to the bad news column. "A business will cost $300,000 at least. One horse for God's sake is over $100 a week to keep. It's worse than a private school." She says if you add up the bad news column at the moment, the $400,000 has almost halved since we came to Sydney. Almost halved in only a few months.

But Winks tells me not to listen to her. He'd still be working in a gravel pit and eating one potato for dinner if he didn't have the savvy to turn one dollar into two. "You've got to spend money to make money," he says. "You've got to move in the right circles and there's no better way to do that than by owning a well-bred horse." He holds the shining shoe away from himself for admiring. "If you want to get to know the right people you've got to look the part," he winks. He says there's no easier way in this world to make money than to spend a sum betting on a racehorse and having that racehorse win and return you two or three times the cash. "There's an art to punting. That art is for you, the punter, to be in the know." He taps his nose with his finger as he says this. "You've got to know where the clever money is going. You've got to move in the right circles and know what horse is carrying the clever dough."

*

My bedroom has a double bed for my bed as if I were an adult, though not an adult like Heels and Winks who have never slept, as far as I've seen, in a double bed but in single beds pushed together to make a vast bed with a gap in the middle. The reason the beds are pushed together is not simply to create one vast bed. The reason, they tell me, is that it benefits Winks' heart. Winks has a defective heart valve and always has had since a bout of something called rheumatic fever that he suffered as a boy. The pushed-together beds allow him to stretch out and sleep without being scrunched up in a way that would mean his heart would be scrunched up and not pump properly and kill him. I'm told a lot of things. If horis are not really animals and a fall from a ladder is not a cure for stuttering but elocution lessons are, if … if … I could go on and on, then why would Winks become a dead man if the single beds weren't pushed together? Winks looks fine to me. He is yet to have more than fifty-seven grey hairs growing through his black hair. I've counted them secretly at dinner: fifty-seven exactly. A paltry number in among the black. His arms are solid with muscle and meshed with plump veins. When he walks I need to skip into a run to match his pace.

Surely a sick man would never have been able to withstand those hotel beatings and deal out beatings of his own.

"That life would have killed me sooner or later," he confides, shaking his head slowly. "It'll be a better life here. Here's the type of place to raise a boy. A clean slate."

A clean slate. Those words, the mix of disappointment and hope in his tone, make my stomach sink and throb as if vomit is about to curdle towards my throat. I wish, oh how I wish, I could have the clean slate I was born with, not this shameful one at twelve years old.

"Even so," he continues, "you never know. I might only live another five years, if that. So be a good boy. Be a good boy because we don't know how much time we'll have left together." He says the last sentence while patting his chest like a patient.

Of course I will be a good boy. I will make the most of this clean slate moving to Australia has given me, I promise. Five years sounds like a long time but it's not really. I would be sixteen and have no father. That's a terrible thing to look forward to at the end of five years. Every day of that five years will be tainted by that knowledge. I don't know whether to reach over to Winks and hug him, my temporary father. Should I begin to cry? Is that what he would want at this moment, to comfort him and him comfort me? No. He holds out his hand for me to shake. "Deal?" he winks, cheerily for a dying man. "You be a good boy and we'll both be happy."

"Deal," I reply.

"That's the way." He slaps me playfully on the knee just as Heels opens the flat's door letting in a farty smell of boiling vegetables from the rest of the building. She has been shopping and carries two packages. One very fat, its brown paper bound by blue stringy ribbon. She throws the packages onto the pouf and begins picking the fat one apart.

"I found the perfect thing," she says almost singing the sentence in her excitement. "Perfect, perfect, perfect."

Winks tells her that we've been having a man-to-man talk about being a good boy. He winks at her.

"I certainly hope you *are* going to be a good boy. In fact I'm positive he will be. Especially after this coming Sunday."

Sunday? What's happening on Sunday? Sunday is always lie-in day. It's do-nothing day. Here in Sydney there is a beach at Coogee where last weekend we ate a cut lunch on the hot sand and got burnt watching the waves curl over onto the shore as if being sliced. I swam in the foam and swallowed salt water. Let's do that again this Sunday. Please, please.

Inside the ripped-apart paper is a navy blue blazer, its sleeves folded neatly like arms. Shiny gold buttons stud the cuffs and front. A red and yellow bow-tie is pinned to the lapel. Heels tears open the other, smaller package—a white shirt in a plastic sheaf cover, a pair of white walk-socks.

"*This* is what's happening on Sunday," Heels says holding the blazer against my body to test the length. "On Sunday you are going to be christened." She stops still a second, stares and frowns into space. "Or is it baptised? What's the term we're supposed to use?" She leans her chin on her fingers, wondering if there's a difference between christened and baptised. Are they the same thing? She doesn't know, nor does Winks. I certainly have no idea. She will have to ask Aunty Dorothy.

Aunty Dorothy is my aunty in name but no relation. She's been Heels' Sydney friend from years before I was born. They met at the Randwick races in the Members near the Champagne Bar when Dorothy was with two forgettable friends who had horses with Tommy Smith that even he, the great trainer himself, couldn't make win. Dorothy was wearing a gold and blue striped turban-style hat arrangement with the thinnest of gold chain banding fastened by a gold gauze brooch in the shape of a rose. "I just had to ask her where she got it," Heels answers if people ask, "So how did you two meet?"

They have euchre nights and oyster mornays at Doyle's where they spend whole afternoons saying, "Beautiful oysters. I can still taste those oysters they were so mouth-watering."

Aunty Dorothy has never been married. She likes to be footloose and fancy-free and can't be bothered with men, though she has been proposed to twice. She suspects they were after her money. She inherited a horse transport business from her father and would rather spend the money on herself and playing euchre with the ladies and going to Doyle's than bother with men.

"She's a ladies' woman," Winks winks.

"What's a ladies' woman?" I ask.

"Enough of that," Heels reprimands him, but the winking continues.

"A ladies' woman is …"

"Don't you dare say such terrible things to the boy."

"A ladies' woman is a *ladies'* woman, son."

"He means a lady who prefers the company of ladies in a closer way than usual," Heels reluctantly explains.

"The way you two natter I wonder sometimes," Winks mumbles.

"That's a disgusting and terrible thing to say."

"She likes to hold your hand when you're walking. What's that all about?"

"How dare you! Girls holding hands is as innocent and natural as men playing their sweaty games together and hugging and putting their heads and hands in all sorts of places in scrums. You don't say *they're* men's men in that disgusting, terrible way."

Aunty Dorothy will know whether the term is christened or baptised because she's Catholic and Catholics are a churchy kind. We don't want to get to church and make fools of ourselves and look like ignorants.

"Am I going to be a Catholic?" I ask.

No, I am not to be made into a Catholic, says Heels. A compromise has been worked out between being a Catholic and the fact that Winks' mother, my grandmother, was a Baptist and Winks himself has been baptised, or christened or whatever it is, a Baptist, and Heels' mother was a Presbyterian. "At least I think it was Presbyterian," she says, chewing her lip.

This is the first time I've heard them mention religion. "Are we religious?" I ask.

Winks screws up his mouth to one side as if biting back laughter.

"Of course we are," Heels answers sternly. "We just don't make a song and dance about it."

"Do we really believe in God?"

"That's a terrible question. Of course we do. Everybody believes in God."

"We don't go to church," I say.

She blinks and admires the blazer, smooths it with her fingers. "It's what's in the heart that counts. Sunday is a difficult day to get to church because it's the day when I relax."

"Do you pray?" I cannot ever recall her praying. I've never

seen her kneel down and put her hands together or say "God" or "Jesus" except as a curse.

"Of course I pray."

"What do you pray for?"

"Lots of things."

"Like what?" I sense the possibility of catching her out.

"Oh I don't know," she sighs, fed up with the conversation. "When we've had one of our horses racing or backed a horse I pray for them to win."

"But they don't always win."

"Maybe they'd lose a lot more if I didn't pray."

"But that's not real praying. It's not praying for forgiveness and peace and love like praying is meant for."

She holds up her hand, sucks the air for me to stop pestering her with ridiculous questions. I say I don't want to be baptised or christened because it's for doing when you're a baby. She says I'm still a baby to her and I will be made a Church of Englander because with the Church of England you get a lot of good old-fashioned ritual and the long robes and organ music like the Catholics and plenty of rules and dos and don'ts for life but without having to become a Catholic. To be a Catholic is to be another type of person altogether. No one can say exactly how being Catholic makes you a different type of person. They, Heels and Winks, are not experts on the ins and outs of religion and don't pretend to be. But Catholics believe in all sorts of strange hooey and have to eat fish on Friday and have a king called a Pope. Being Church of England is in the middle of being Catholic and being Presbyterian or one of those Baptists who hold their services in halls for goodness' sake. What's the point of going to church if you're not going into a nice church but into a common hall?

I am going to be christened or baptised or whatever it is and that's that. There will be no arguments on the matter. No ifs and buts. Aunty Dorothy is quite right when she says, What can you expect of a child who has not been received into a church? It's like jinxing them, setting them up for trouble. "You've certainly been proof of that," says Heels.

What's more, if I'm to get into a top school in Sydney, somewhere with genuine class that will open doors for me in the world, how will it look if I'm asked what religion I am and I can't tick any box. They'd show us out the way we came in. I should have been done years ago but time just slipped away and besides, there were no nice churches in Heritage. None like the Church of England church up the road in Kensington, St Martin's. It's nice in there. It's not too grand and not too gloomy as to make the whole occasion depressing. We want it to be a happy affair. There's a lovely garden out front to take photos in. So I must look smart in my new blazer, and if the Minister fellow or whatever he's called, the Father, the Reverend, asks if I've done Sunday School lessons and studied the bible I'm to say, Yes, because that's what he's been told. Now go try on the new blazer.

*

Greeks are pakehas but not quite, I decide. I inspect their skin, mine versus theirs. The pink-white-tan of mine on my forearms has no oily colour in it as in theirs. This effect on the skin, this oily colour, creates a grey misty smear under the surface where the dark hairs sprout, each hair spaced wider than the fine, red-blond hairs on my forearm. This grey misty smear makes the skin on Stephen Papadopoulos's arms appear transparent for the first few layers like Vaseline or Vicks VapoRub. "Olive," Stephen says. "The colour's olive." It's a cloudy, grey-blue tinged whiteness that surely is close enough to pakeha to pass for pakeha. Winks' skin is darker than Heels'. It has a permanent light tan but would never be mistaken for hori because it's merely his tendency to go brown instantly a ray of sun touches him. "I wouldn't have married him if it was anything else," says Heels. But Stephen's darkening, his "olive", is certainly a different kind of pakeha tint.

"European," says Stephen when I ask him, What's a Greek, and where does a Greek come from? He's as good as pakeha, definitely, I'm sure of it. Heels wants me to tell her about my new school. She hopes I've made a nice friend, someone nice and suitable that I can bring home to meet her and Winks and play with as long as we're not too rowdy and can keep to ourselves because there isn't much room. I answer by making a joke about trying to say Stephen's name, how it's just as well I don't stutter anymore because how would I be able to attempt the name Stephen Papadopoulos if I stuttered. I can't even pronounce it anyway and have to settle for Stephen With The Name No One Can Say. Stephen has been assigned by the teacher to be my guide and new friend at the primary school at Randwick until I can look after myself. He's my Clean Slate Friend, I've decided, the first friend of my new, clean life. He's my best friend because he knows nothing about me and therefore I don't have to dislike him. For all he knows I'm equal to him. When I ask him slyly, just slipping it casually into conversation, what kind of bad things he has done in his life he doesn't really know what I mean. His brown bulgy eyes dart left to right, right to left, confused by the question, by the idea of *bad things*. I asked him the question to make sure he isn't like me. He's better than me, and therefore he makes *me* better, he keeps my clean slate clean by his presence. If he knew about bad things, if he had done them himself I would have to find another friend whom I could look up to. I even single out particular bad things for Stephen to consider, a test, shrugging and sticking out my bottom lip as though these particular bad things, by complete chance, have only now leapt into my head: "Getting drunk for instance. Or thieving. Thieving from your parents."

His bug-eyes stare blankly from their sockets at nothing, then close in a frown, a wince of distaste as if even thinking about those sorts of questions is a dirty act. He makes me feel dirty. I should hate him for that, but how sweet it is to know and be considered by him and everyone else at school his equal, the boy he is helping be orientated and settled in at school.

Stephen's ugliness makes him even more wholesome. His mouth is upturned in a constant smile because his two front teeth poke out and down and across his bottom lip. His top lip appears thicker than it really is because it is stretched over those teeth like over a mouthguard. His lips can't close. The gap between his teeth is so big he can almost jam his tongue through it as a trick. He smells of the boiled vegetable fart smell of Randwick. The air of the place, the streets, the stairs and passageways where I live reek at night of cabbage cooking. With Stephen the smell comes through his skin and his breath. If he speaks up close to me I gag from what he calls garlic. His fingertips have a sticky, rubber texture—when he was first made to shake my hand in introduction by the teacher this odour, this garlic, rubbed off onto my skin.

"We didn't come to Australia to mix with Greeks," says Heels. I explain to her that I have looked really closely at Stephen's skin and as far as I can tell it's pakeha skin. Different colour arm-hairs, yes. But olive is just a greyer tint of my own arm colour. And anyway, Winks' skin is darker than Stephen's.

She doesn't want an argument on the matter. "Look at this gizmo," she says to change the subject. "Have you ever seen the likes?" It's a cardboard box. "Somewhere in here, if I can work out how to get to it, is a bag." She peers for the place to tear the box open. "It's called a wine cask."

I persist with reporting on Stephen's skin colour, how he doesn't have a single freckle. I have freckles everywhere on my skin but he has perfect, undark skin.

"It's not just about skin," Heels responds, digging at the wine cask with her thumbnail.

"What is it then?"

"Well, you know …" She doesn't finish the sentence.

"No I *don't* know."

"They're, you know, different."

"How?"

"They just are."

"Different in the way Catholics are a different type of person?"

"Yes. No. Even more so."

"How?"

"It's obvious."

"How?"

She takes a deep exasperated breath and says it's hard to put into words exactly all of what she means but it has something to do with *standards*. It's to do with standards of basic things such as how one presents oneself, one's clothes and one's grooming. One's hygiene, one's tidiness. All that plus if you don't speak the same language as them you're not on the same wavelength. You can't blame them for that, for their language, it's just the way it is. Not that she's saying this Stephen person and his family and his type of people are down there with horis.

She tugs and twists the wine-cask teat into position to pour and says she can't be bothered talking about the subject anymore. She's made herself quite clear on the matter and wants to relax with a glass of cold white wine and a cigarette. So no more talk about this skin colour or that skin colour and freckles. It's enough to put her off her drink. And no more using the word *pakeha* now that we're in *this* country. And do get a *proper* friend, one of our kind. This school I'm currently in, I'll just have to grin and bear until they can get me into a decent school. I'm to consider where I am now as a holding pattern where I must do as well as I can with my schooling, obey the teachers and impress the right people at the right schools for next year. In the meantime, yes, I will have to mix in circles that I can't avoid but I don't have to bring them home and have them in her house.

Stephen is what's called a Greek Cypriot. He lives in Australia because his parents couldn't live where they come from, Cyprus, because they feared they'd be harmed by the other kind of Cypriots, the Turk Cypriots. These Turk Cypriots lived in slums and were no better than dogs, he sneers. They would kill him, his parents and all his relations at the drop of a hat. The Turkish Cypriots want to take over Cyprus and have it as theirs, even though there was only a fraction of them in Cyprus compared to the Greek people.

His father came to Australia with nothing, *nothing*, but now he owns a fruit and vegetable shop and house and a car and trailer. Stephen tells me this very proudly.

Another boy, Jonathan Jonathan—his last name the same as his first for some reason that is never explained—is a long way from being pakeha, yet for all his brown skin he has fine pakeha features, a sharp end on his nose and a square chin. He escaped from Iraq because the new President there, Bakr, led a coup which his father opposed, and his uncles too, three of whom were killed. Jonathan Jonathan and Stephen seldom smile when they're together. They talk about how they wish they weren't in Australia but at home on their ancestors' soil where their blood is, the blood of their kin which has been spilt and should be avenged and one day hopefully will be by them. Stephen and Jonathan Jonathan say I couldn't possibly be expected to understand what they are talking about—leaving a country because you fear you'll be killed; having to live there in the first place among people who are no better than dogs as their families had to live.

Stephen seems much older suddenly, grown up, his lips pursed over his protruding teeth, one end of his top lip curled in a sneer. He's no longer the wholesome boy who considered me his equal. He's behaving as if he's superior to me. Who is he to think he's superior to me as he clearly does with his "Anglos like you know nothing," spitting the word "nothing" just as he spits the words "dogs" and "Turks"? I want him back as my equal, his arm around my shoulder, mine around his, secretly wanting to kiss his bucked mouth in the way it feels good to imagine pecking the mouths of girls I get a crush on.

I *do* understand what they mean, I say, putting a higher pitch in my voice to create the effect of being a little offended. My family had to escape the Maoris who were dogs as well and were taking over even though there was more of us than them just like with the Turks. I don't mention the sale of the Heritage Hotel for $400,000. I say my family left New Zealand with nothing, *nothing*, just as Stephen's family and Jonathan Jonathan's family had left their countries with nothing.

They nod their understanding of my understanding. They nod their sympathy and sit silent on the playground bench. Jonathan Jonathan says he would invite us both over to his place on the weekend but his father only allows Iraqis in his house. Stephen says it's the same for him at his house with Greeks. I say there's no such rule at my house. Both of them would be very welcome there. They say they envy me that. Very welcome, but the problem is our flat is too small for visitors because we're so poor. Perhaps the best thing to do would be for us to meet down at Coogee and do something together, though not this Sunday. This Sunday I have to be baptised or christened because in New Zealand there were no churches or religion. Religion was banned by the Maoris which is another reason my family and I came to Australia, to stop being persecuted for our religion.

So many lies in just a few seconds. All of them black marks on my clean slate. I vow to start my clean slate again, from this very moment. I worry how many times I can start a clean slate over.

To become a soldier of Christ you don't wear a soldier uniform. It's a different war from Vietnam on the news with its burning trees, its Americans. Very different from the World War II of drinkers at the Heritage Hotel, rows of medals across their suit fronts for Anzac Day, merry and drunk as if at the races. Christ's war is a war against being a bad person, Aunty Dorothy explains. It's yourself at war with yourself. It's a war of souls. What is a soul? A soul is something, well, no one can say exactly. Think of it as a tiny pocket of air or gas made up of information about you that gets stored up inside you, all the information about your life, what you've done and should not have done. When you die this tiny pocket floats away, up, up, into space, past the stars, across to what we call The Other Side. There the information can be deciphered by angels to see if you're a fit and proper person to enter Heaven.

Can it ever be wiped clean, this information? Can bits of information be scrubbed out to give you a second chance, a third chance, fourth chance, fifth, sixth?

Yes they can. When that happens it is called God's mercy

letting you off the hook if you promise to change and you pray. The start of this war is called the baptism and for this occasion you must wear your best clothes, those new clothes of yours, the blazer, the white shirt, white socks from the brown packages. No bow-tie though. I beg for no bow-tie and am granted a compromise to wear my collar buttoned up instead. My hair is slicked to the side. My black shoes glow from Heels' elbow grease.

Aunty Dorothy's church uniform, every bit of which is white except the gold chain with a *t* hanging from it at her throat, includes a big-brimmed hat turned up at one side in what she calls a slouch-hat arrangement. A lace handkerchief is tucked inside her watchband for weeping. Just as well, for her eye corners are welling up and mixing with mascara as she leads me into the church's dark, wood cave where daylight is like twilight—orange and blurry red through the picture-book windows.

This is my first time in such a place and she, who knows about religion, has the privilege of leading me forward. The honour of feeling my hand press around hers because I'm scared of the horror-movie organ music. I have a shivering sense of being watched, not by some single pair of human eyes, or the human eyes of families in rows of benches, but by God-eyes, Jesus-eyes, Angel-eyes invisible in the air with the power of x-ray judgments that make their owners angry and offended to see me in this place, me with my clean slate dirty.

Along the rear bench, the shiny board-seats Aunty Dorothy calls pews, a baby wrapped in a white shawl begins bawling in its mother's rocking arms as if being hurt. Beside it another baby joins in with a shriek like a screamed warning.

I refuse to take another step. I pull away from Aunty Dorothy to run back into the bright outside. Winks blocks me, grapples my flailing arms until he fastens them in his grip out in front of me. Heels shuffles away from the scene pretending to search for something in her purse, letting Aunty Dorothy smooth my hair down with lick-spit as if my real mother and hush me with "Here's the Minister. Straighten up. Be a good boy." She twists in the direction of the altar's gold crucifix and apologises to it with a flick of fingers across her breasts, "Forgive us."

Winks pushes me down into the pews beside the howling infants as the Minister approaches, his hands suddenly appearing out of hidden sleeves in his white poncho. He speaks, not with words but with a slow passing of his pale hands across the air, directing me to line up over there at the bubbler or is it a birdbath? He then slips his hands into the poncho sleeves and walks in slow motion as if in a trance to the place where we all must stand, the mothers and their babies, fathers, Aunty Dorothy, Heels, Winks, me.

*

It's as if he's washing the baby's hair. From the cup of his palm the Minister tips water from the birdbath over the first baby's bald, blue-veined skull. The baby's face squeezes into toothless screams as if in terrible pain, as if the water is too hot or too cold or not water at all but acid. Yet the Minister keeps cupping and tipping, expressionless, then makes a crisscross sign on the baby's forehead. He mumbles something I can't quite hear, repeating the crisscrossing motion with his thumb, down and across, down and across. Now for the second baby. It shudders and screams as if suffering greatly. The Minister's actions are gentle, and the mother's shshshing soft, yet how can they be so cruel as not even to flinch at the baby's cries?

Now for me. Step forward, the Minister signals with his dripping hand. Step forward. Come closer to the water, this water that has been purified in Christ's name and therefore when it touches me I shall be purified in this act of baptism. Bend to the water, please. It is cool and tickling running through my hair from his fingers. In Christ's name manfully fight under his banner against sin, the world and the devil. Continue as Christ's faithful soldier and servant until your life's end, for you are received into the congregation of Christ's flock and are signed now with the sign of the cross upon which Christ suffered for our sins. Down and across, down and across. The Minister's wet thumb slides down and across my forehead as if writing in code with the invisible ink of water. Christ died for our sins? He is like one of those hero soldiers, Victoria Cross winners who died to save their comrades.

The water cross the Minister has made on my skin becomes chillier as it picks up the slightest draught. Goose-flesh creeps over my body. The water cross becomes so burning-cold I'm sure it must be a brand he has made with his thumb, as animals are branded with initials and numbers to mark ownership and year of birth. Water from the bird-bath is trickling down my neck but the brand on my forehead is the water that matters. It's the sign that Christ was here. A sign that I have been accepted and stamped ready for war as his soldier.

The Minister passes me a white hand-towel to dry myself. He dries his own hands with his own towel then slips them into his sleeves all the way up to his elbows for slow walking towards the picture-window above the altar where Christ stands in ancient-style clothes, a robe and sandals, surrounded by orange and red panes, his palms open and held out to welcome me and all the rest of his soldiers including the two babies though they'd have to wait years to be of any use as soldiers. The gold cross on a pole below Christ's window gleams like a sword hilt. "Let us pray," the Minister says, bowing his head.

There are miniature cushions on the floor under the seats. Slip off the bony pews onto your knees and put the cushion under your kneecaps so it's more comfy, Aunty Dorothy whispers. Close your eyes and lower your head. No need to make a steeple with your fingers, that looks silly. I obey her and pass the instructions on to Heels and Winks, my left eye peeping open to make sure they're doing what they're told. They're not. Heels leans on the pew in front of her to avoid kneeling, Winks has placed one knee on a cushion but refuses to kneel all the way or bow his head. Kneeling, bowing and scraping go against a man's grain, he frowns. He's not too keen on this bowing and scraping business.

"Kneel down," I plead with wide-opened eyes.

"I'll ladder my stocking," Heels mouths.

Winks relents but won't close his eyes past a squint.

"Kneel down," I demand of Heels.

She tugs the cushion away from Winks' knees and stacks it on her own cushion for extra padding then lowers herself. She closes her eyes, not in prayer but because she's expecting a great tearing.

Christ's blessing be upon you all, the Minister says in a sing-song way. Amen.

Aunty Dorothy nudges me to repeat the Amen. My left eye checks Winks. Amen, he nods. Heels winces an Amen, pushing herself up and back to safety.

The Minister: "Open your hymn books."

The hymn books lie on the backs of the pews in front of us. They are no ordinary books. They have brown leather importance and shiny pages more like ribbon than paper. The thee and thou lyrics are poems impossible to understand. God in three persons, blessed trinity. Holy, holy, holy, all the saints adore thee, casting down their golden crowns around the glassy seas.

Winks sings with no sound, barely moving his lips. Heels and Aunty Dorothy sing in shaky, shrill girl voices. Aunty Dorothy is louder. She takes deep breaths between the lines for more singing power and is able to direct her singing towards the altar and Jesus-window because she knows some of the lines by heart and can look up from the book. I sing "Holy, holy, holy" in full voice then mime the rest while attempting to decode the meaning of the phrase "casting down their golden crowns".

More kneeling and bowing, more praying. This time the congregation joins in a chant, a low unified mutter of deep respectfulness. For this chant, which is like a hymn without music, no one uses a book. Everyone knows the words except me. Even for Heels and Winks the words come automatically. *Them?* Now me. *Me?* Somehow the phrases arrive in my mouth. Had they seeped their way from the world into my memory without my knowing? Or is it a miracle of baptism? "Hallowed be thy name. Thy kingdom come. Thy will be done on earth as it is in Heaven. Give us this day our daily bread."

Bread. There is such a thing as bread that is not bread but the flesh of Christ. There is wine that is not really wine but the blood of Christ. The bread is eaten and the wine is drunk in a little meal called communion at the altar near the sword hilt and directly under the Jesus-window. This must truly be the moment when I become a soldier of Christ because it sounds to me like an initiation test, an obstacle course of sorts just as they have in the army. I will take the test alone. Winks mumbles that he'll be fine sitting right where he is. "I'm not a wine drinker anyway," he cracks to Heels who gives him the elbow and says to me, "You go up and do it by yourself like a big boy. I've got my stockings to think about."

Aunty Dorothy won't go with me because it's not appropriate, her being Catholic at a Church of England communion.

"On the night he was betrayed," the Minister says with his hands out of his sleeves and held away from his body as if feeling for rain. The bread-flesh and the wine-blood are a way of eating and drinking Christ because Christ himself said as much at a dinner when the betrayal happened. I don't know exactly what betrayal that was but it makes sense that a great military leader had his enemies. That's the whole point of a war. Just why we're required to eat flesh and drink blood I can't say. That's cannibalism which the horis are supposed to have done to each other before the pakehas brought civilised order to New Zealand. This pakeha cannibalism has been kept a secret from me. This bread-flesh and wine-blood is surely my initiation into the war of souls. A war that has its fair share of bleeding and gore by the sounds of it—Christ hanging from the Cross from nails for a start. If I can swallow and gulp what I'm told is flesh and blood and not faint or throw up at the sight of it I will have passed the test. That must be the whole point of communion.

But why will I, of all people, be given alcohol? Isn't there something apart from wine that could be used? By calling wine blood am I expected to be turned off liquor for life? Is what is called wine here really real blood?

"Body of Christ," the Minister says, placing the crusty flesh on my tongue and moving down the line of six kneelers to the next opened mouth. When he reaches the end of the line he goes back to the first person and offers them a wine glass to sip from, grey metal not glass. After they've sipped he wipes the rim with a napkin. "Blood of Christ."

He puts the metal glass to my lips. I've not swallowed the bread-flesh and am not ready to drink. I don't want to swallow the flesh. It's rough on my tongue, flavourless, a disgusting thing to have in the mouth, Christ or no Christ. I want to spit it out. But this is a test. The Minister holds the grey glass till it touches my lips. "Blood of Christ," he repeats firmly. I swallow the crust. I sip the wine. The wine tastes nothing like the sweet syrup of the phone box. It's sour like a medicine meant to cure. Christ has turned his blood into this alcohol to cure me of ever wanting alcohol again.

I have passed Christ's test. I have pieces of him inside my stomach. I am carrying Christ inside my body. Christ was the son of God who created and rules everything, everyone. I am the part-son of God.

RANDWICK ROADS TURN INTO a paddock-circle with a rim of green grass and centre of gravel and sand. It's not part of a farm though the Members grandstand has pretty fringes as grand homesteads of another time do. The grandstand wears iron lace and fronts onto vast lawns with flower-bed borders. The horses don't draw ploughshares. They've no thick, hairy draught-horse ankles and jaws but velvet coats that ripple when they walk. Their heads hang eight feet tall in the air yet for being such giants these horses are lean and very delicate, ballet-stepping on the spot. They have a mysterious mark on them as all horses do. God's mark, I decide. I'm sure of it. A woody scab on the inside of their front legs that never goes away. It's called a chestnut. I have no idea why. I've heard it told that a great artist once took a hammer to his *David* because the sculpture was so perfect he thought a bang on the knee would bring it to life. I expect God did that with horses and that's their chestnut.

In this part of Randwick there is no boiled cabbage smell. There is farm smell, a horse smell of the earth, the dung of a great beast. One of God's smells. Others I consider God smells are cow-smell, sheep, cut grass, wood smoke. The not-God smells are rubber, especially burning rubber, petrol, perfume, hairspray and bleach. There's no proof that one smell is godly and one isn't, but what else am I to think when I, a fully baptised piece of God, should find it impossible not to stop and inhale horse-smell in the air. The oats and chaff, lucerne and bran composted in a horse's insides, a fuming brown-green porridge on the ground. Purifying is the word. It probably has the power to purify concrete when smeared there by hooves and human shoes. Purify it and make it honorary grass.

Those ungodly smells make my eyes water and sting, my nose run. I accept that my prayers may get God's ear but not necessarily a response. Aunty Dorothy calls this "testing one's faith". Heels calls it "playing hard to get". Perhaps my sensitivity to smells is the way God communicates with me.

It's Saturday. We're getting ready for the races. I'm tall enough and old enough to wear Winks' fawn and brown check jacket now that he's put on a few pounds and can't fit into it. I've reached a point where something must be said. I must tell Winks that his Brylcreem and aftershave are ungodly smells. I must tell Heels that the perfume she calls Duty Free and VO5 are disgusting to me. I will no longer be able to kiss her or be hugged by her unless she stops spraying her hair stiff and squirting Duty Free over herself. I am a piece of God and fighting his war, therefore causing my eyes and nostrils to burn and swell is to cause pain to God.

"I'm not going to be told what to do by a twelve-year-old, thank you very much," she says with a mocking puff of her cheeks. She laughs to Winks. "We've got a preacher on our hands. One who wants us to stink. Whoever heard of such nonsense. 'Hairspray'. 'Piece of God'." She juts her jaw to me: "And don't start with your 'I don't want to go to the races' or look out. You're coming and that's that."

Winks parts his hair to the skin, laughs into the wardrobe mirror and jokes "I'll have Yorkshire pudding with that beef, please," watching her reflection twist this way and that until her dress clears her hips. She pokes her tongue out for extra strength for the final tug. She asks me to zip her tight as a drum across her shoulder blades. A tree-shape of creased skin forms above the zipper. There's a similar tree at the front above her breasts. Winks pats aftershave on his shiny chin and steps away from the mirror to let Heels start on her face.

She writes her top lip into an M with red lipstick and the bottom one into a U, then steps to one side for Winks. It's their race-day system. He flicks his tie into a knot, buttons his tan waistcoat and yanks it down over his protruding belly. She leans right up to the glass and blackens her lashes into upturned hooks, plucks and pencils two ginger eyebrows into place on her forehead. He pulls his suit-coat lapel forward then bucks it off his shoulders and pulls it forward again until its weight is settled evenly across him. She paints her fingertips red with a tiny brush and holds them clear of everything like a surgeon. He pushes a black porkpie hat very slowly onto his head, takes it off, strokes its green feather smooth, puts the hat on again. He does this three times. She pins either a white carnation or a red rose or sprig of lilac into his lapel. He takes a roll of cash from inside his coat and removes the rubber band that binds it. He counts the money into two piles: one hundred, three hundred, seven hundred, a thousand dollars in one pile. Fifty, seventy, eighty, one hundred in the other. He gives the one hundred to Heels. "That enough, love?" She calls it chicken-feed so he counts out some more and tells her to go easy on the firewater because it's a hot day. She tells him to mind his own business and concentrate on backing a winner not on lecturing her. He says he's got the good oil on two certainties that weren't trying last start. He worries about pickpockets so his money is divided into three lots. One for tucking inside his coat. One for his back pocket. One in the side pocket beneath his handkerchief. In case he has a bad day on the punt he folds a twenty-dollar bill into his sock for cab fare home. Heels inspects that his hat is tilted at a nice angle. He makes sure her teeth are clear of lipstick. She cleans them with a rub of her pinkie and says, "OK God, let us play" for the benefit of me the preacher-man. Not even a man, but a half-man. A boy.

*

The bible I've been reading, the white leather one with gold cross on the cover, was a baptism present from Aunty Dorothy. It says the best way to live is to be poor. The worst way is to be rich. In its pictures the people have long hair and beards like the demonstrators on TV, the bludgers, drug-takers and layabouts I'm not allowed to be when I grow up. Money changers are particularly frowned upon in the bible. The bible is designed to turn me against everything I know. Just as Heels and Winks turned me against horis and Heritage and Greeks, the bible is turning me against the rest. It would turn me against my new uncles. They aren't related to me but are my uncles nonetheless because they're friends of Winks and to a lesser extent Heels. Are they money changers? They certainly seem to be. They stand on boxes at the races at a place called The Rails between the public area and fenced-off

Members. They twiddle a venetian blind of numbers and carry over their shoulders a big doctor's bag full of money. Uncle Keith, Uncle Chicka, Uncle Jack. They yell "five thousand to two thousand, Gourmet Guest. Eight hundred to two hundred, Engine Room. Two to one the favourite, Beez Neez. In from sixes to fours, Sir Simeon" a minute before a race begins. Punters push forward waving cash. They bellow bets or mouth a horse's name and signal with their fingers to add a one-thousand or two-thousand dollar wager to their tab. My uncles record the bets with a furious scribble on the top card of a deck of cards. Their pens are a blue or red crayon stick. Just what they scribble only they can understand.

The bible has turned me against horseracing itself. I wish I could forget about God. I love the racing, the bugle calling horses to canter to the barriers. The earthquake of hooves. When cheerers in the grandstand stomp and scream home the winner their guttural madness thrills me. I scream and stomp with them until breathless and emptied out. I stand close to the horses as they jig-jog to be hosed down, their ribs heaving, skin foaming and covered in a net of fat veins. They shake their bodies like a wet dog and sweat-foam sprays onto me and smells like freshly turned soil. So does the snot from their snorting. I wish I could forget about God, but that can't be. For these are God's animal athletes and look at what is being done to them. Their tongues are black-purple and bleeding because a length of women's pantyhose has been used to tie them to their jaws like a tourniquet. Why do they do that? I ask Winks. Because jockeys lose control of horses whose tongues work up over the bit, that's why, he says. The cap-gun whipping infuriates me. Those wizen-faced child-men have no right to hit God's athletes. Someone must stop them grinding their spurs along the horses' flanks. Winks knows the jockeys, the trainers. He can do something. I'll find him this minute and tell him to do something and do it now.

The Members Bar. Race Five. Time of the day when men take women by the waist. Not to dance but to rub their hollows and see how long they're allowed to keep their hand there. The women are much younger than the men. They teeter on heel-spikes and glance about for who is and isn't looking at them. Their dresses are yellow, pink, powder-blue, and hang like singlets from their narrow, brown shoulders. Their brown backs are exposed. They're not wearing bras though some have a white skin stripe where a bra would be. All but the tips of their breasts show. The shapes of their nipples point through.

Drink must have made the men forget who they are. Surely in a minute they'll remember they have hairs sprouting on their ears and noses. They have holes of old blackheads there too. Each hole contains a bubble of perspiration. How ugly they must seem to these beautiful women! Yet they're allowed to keep their crinkly hands where they do, rubbing up and down, then resting, rubbing up and down, then resting. The men try to squeeze the women closer to them, and the women eventually give in with giggling and granny-steps. The men wear gold wedding rings but these are not their wives. Their wives are as old as Heels and don't come to the races, or if they do they spend the day at the Ladies Lunch by invitation of the race club Chairman as Heels is doing now.

But *these* women—how much older are they than me? Only ten years older, maybe nine. They allow the men to lower their hands and stroke a buttock quickly before returning to the waist. The men whisper into their ears and the women laugh. They call the women "girlie" and ask them their names—Nicola and Angela, Mandy, Caroline, Meg— but keep calling them girlie as if they weren't listening to the answer. Some of these women are the same girlies as last weekend. Some Saturdays there are new Nicolas, Angelas, Mandys, Carolines, Megs sipping through straws such drinks that lemon peels stick out of in the shape of wings. They smirk at each other. Sometimes one will roll her eyes when the man she's with isn't looking. They take off their bee-keeper hats with gauze veils by drawing out a long pin like string. Once the hat's detached they place it on a stool behind them and shake their long hair down. The men inhale deeply and say, "I smell apples. You use apples for shampoo?"

The men forget to keep their voices low. Ears are flapping. My ears are flapping as I push past looking for Winks. They probably think I'm too young to understand. But I under- stand. I understand there'd be a scene if their wives knew what they were saying, I know that. Not the business talk so much—how they import kitchenware or diagnostic equip- ment for a living, or how they're in the law and have been offered a position on the bench, following up with "asked to be a judge" when met with a blank look from their girlie— but where that kind of talk leads. It leads to money talk—how their turnover has reached two million a year, how money can buy racehorses, cars, holiday houses, but can't buy hap- piness. How they and their wife don't talk anymore. How they've become distant over the years, have grown apart, theirs is a marriage in name only. This is the kind of talk Winks scoffs at with a dismissive hand-wave as "piss-talk" and "the John Thomas talking" and "old men making fools of themselves".

The men tell the girlies they're going on a trip some-where, to Hawaii, next month to chew over their lives. "Have you ever been to Hawaii?" they ask the girlies.

"No," the girlies answer.

"Wonderful place. Sensational weather. The beach—you just do nothing all day."

"Fingers crossed I'll get there some time."

"You should come along and keep me company."

"How on earth can I afford Hawaii!"

"I tell you what. Albert McKenna—lovely fellow Albert—he's got a good horse in the next race. Today's the day its foot's supposed to be on the till. How about I back it and if it wins then that's your plane ticket to Hawaii?"

I can hear Winks' raspy laughing. I stand on tip-toes. He's over there, his slicked black hair with fifty-seven greys nod-ding and tossing back in good humour. He must be having a good day, a winning day. I shuffle sideways between hips and elbows. He's drinking in a group of five: three women, a man I don't know and him. The man I don't know is leaning on the edge of a stool in a way that lets him cross one ankle against the other as he stands. The woman he's with is seated on the stool. He speaks to her an inch away from her ear then cranes to the left at the end of each sentence to look her in the face and smile. She cradles her glass of champagne which has a strawberry floating in the fizz and smiles back at him. The other two women stand on either side of Winks. If this wasn't Winks I'd swear they were girlies. They have those singlet dresses and hollows the girlies have. One of them is resting a hand on Winks' shoulder and using her fingertips to comb her hair from her eyes. "Wow," she responds to what he's telling her. The other woman says "Fantastic" and touches his shirt cuff. He's lying that he sold the Heritage Hotel for two million dollars.

"Two million dollars. I didn't think there'd be two million dollars in the whole of New Zealand let alone for one little hotel," the girlie who is leaning on his shoulder says.

"It wasn't that little," Winks laughs.

"Two million dollars. Gee. What's it like to be a multi-millionaire?"

"It's no big deal," he shrugs, beaming and swallowing his Adam's apple. He's peeping down her front and trying to disguise it from her by blinking quickly. She's following his eyeline down to her breast ends, up, down, up. She clearly doesn't mind him looking there. She breathes deeper to make her breasts puff out. She and the girlie on the other side of him nuzzle against his arms as a signal for him to put his arm around both of them, which he does. He begins to rub the hollows of their backs. Down, down, across the bum of the shoulder girlie. Back to the hollow, down to one buttock then across the other, then back up.

"Dad," I say through clenched teeth, pulling on his sleeve, pulling his hand away from the shoulder girlie's hollow. "Dad. Come here," I demand, barely audible, seething. He drops his hands to his sides and turns. "Oh," he chuckles awkwardly. "How are you?" He explains to the girlies that I'm his son. I don't look at him or them. I stare at the floor and step backward, turn and walk away a few strides and stop as a sign for Winks to follow. I stand still, fists clenched in my pockets. He pats me on the arm then puts his hands in his pockets too, leaning forward on his toes as if to speak confidentially. I glance at his face and see that there is a look in it I have never seen in Winks before. It's a look I'm certain is fear. A red fear in his cheeks. A white fear in his wide-eyed eyes. His bottom lip trembles. He's trying to hold open a smile that he does not mean. His breathing is quick and beery. "How you going?" he asks. "What can I do for you?"

I don't reply. I refuse to look at him.

"What do you want?" No reply from me. "Say something."

He lifts my chin on his fingertips but I keep my eyes focused anywhere but on him. I jerk my chin free of his touch.

"What's this about?" he asks, frowning. No reply. "What's all this silent treatment about?" He attempts to lift my chin again but I brace to keep my chin where it is. "What sort of antic is this?" he wants to know. "I hope you weren't standing there checking on me, were you?" His voice has become lower, quieter, threatening. "Were you?"

I shake my head, No, and barely parting my lips say I wanted him to stop the whipping of the horses and the tying of their tongues down and kicking them with spurs.

Winks lets out a grunt through his nose. "Jesus son. Don't you think you're taking this religious stuff a bit bloody far?" He brushes my chin playfully with his knuckles. "Listen, old pal. I hope you don't think I was slinging my hook here. Ay? Is that what this is about sour-puss? You think I was slinging my hook?" I remain clenched in silence. "Well you've got the wrong end of the stick there. Too much imagination," he says, tapping his finger on my crown. "I hope you're not going to run off and say that to your mother, that I was slinging my hook. Ay?"

He tells me to listen carefully to him: *they're* just a couple of girlies trying it on. He reckons I should be proud my old man can still pull the birds. It's flattering. I wouldn't begrudge my old man that, would I? He tells me to come on, take that scowl off my face. We men have got to look after each other, keep this sort of business to ourselves. He promises he'll do what he can to raise the matter of the whipping and the tongues and spurs but I know he's just saying that. He winks and says word is Alarm Bells is a cert in the next. Here's a fiver. Go have a bet on Alarm Bells with Uncle Chicka. Buy a pie and a can of soft drink and have a bet. Alarm Bells, number six.

He makes me take a hand out of my pocket and tucks the money into my fist. He takes me by the arm and urges me to go on my way. He gives me a gentle push to make my legs work. I look over my shoulder at him and squeeze between drinkers. He smiles and salutes one finger onto his brow. He salutes again as I pause and watch him. The girlies stare at me, expressionless. They're bored waiting for Winks to rejoin them, which he does now, reaching over to the bar for his beer. The shoulder girlie arches her hand to his shoulder. He peers to see where I am in the bar. He's lost sight of me as I weave and bob. And now I've lost sight of him and am glad of that. I don't want to see again his hand in the girlies' hollows and across their buttocks.

Will he be asking them to go to Hawaii? Will he be saying he and Heels don't talk anymore? That would be the John Thomas talking, for they talk all right. They talk about how the hotel business is the only business they know. They talk about whether to buy a pub they've seen in Kirribilli, such a classy area, such a classy clientele, not a hori in sight. But will my phone box problem come back to haunt them?

They argue my faults never came from *their* side of the family. They talk about how Sydney High School is a selective school. They wish I was smart enough to get into such a school when exams are held later in the year. Wouldn't that be a coup. That would be a feather in their cap to have a son good enough for such a school. It would save them oodles of dollars. There is no indication I am in that league. That's the big league. If I were a racehorse they'd judge me to be something of a plodder. Not a Group One contender at all. "He must take after your side of the family," mutters Heels. Then she blames Heritage, its go-nowhere schools. Money will have to be put aside for one of those schools with grand English-sounding names, for Kings or Knox. For Cranbrook or Shore.

If she knew what was happening in the Members Bar between Winks and the girlies, if I told her what was happening, there'd be talk all right. There'd be yelling-talk, I bet. There'd be sucking and scratching the air talk from her. Pleading and sorry talk from him. There'd be "I'm going for a walk around the block" talk from him while she cries until he closes the door behind him. She'd have a glass of wine and talk to herself bitterly about *men* then cry on cue the moment she hears his key in the lock, and keep crying into her hankie until he insists on taking her out to dinner and she says No a few times before saying Yes and going into the bathroom to re-do her face.

Their marriage might end if she knew what was happening in the Members Bar. He'd leave to wherever he'd leave to, and I'd stay with Heels and her hairspray and hatreds until a new man comes on the scene, a father who's not my father, and me a son who is not his son.

I won't tell her about the Members Bar. But this five dollars. I've been told to keep quiet for five dollars. I'm worth more than that little sum. I must give the money back to Winks. That will be his punishment: I will refuse to play the game and take part in any man-to-man understanding.

There he is, still rubbing the girlies' hollows. He's laughing into their ears and whispering. They flick back their hair to remove any obstruction to his laughing and whispering. "Dad." I tug his sleeve. "Here's your five dollars." He drops his hands to his sides. That look is back on his face: the red fear, the white fear, the trying-to smile. I jam the money into his fingers and hurry away through the drinkers before he tries to charm me with his "You wouldn't tell on your old man, would you? Come on, son. You wouldn't deny your old man some fun."

I sit on the very top seat of the Members grandstand, Ferris-wheel high. For three hours, four hours, I sit there until the insect people below begin to leave the course and the sky, swimming-pool blue all day, begins to dim for evening. The loudspeaker calls for me to make myself known to the nearest policeman because my parents are worried. It calls again and again but I'm making Winks wait. I'm letting him fret on what has become of me. Let him fret on what trouble I may cause him.

The white-coat who mans the glass doors behind me taps me on the shoulder and asks if I'm me, the boy they're calling for on the loudspeaker. He asks if I'm deaf or something and if I'm going to be a nice fellow and come with him to the police.

*

Yet there is no yelling talk or even any sorry talk between them. Winks grazes my chin gently with his knuckle. "I had a feeling you'd tell on me so I told your mother everything."

Heels comes close and speaks stale wine into my face. "And so he should tell on you, shouldn't you my little baby?" she pouts, pinching my chin and calling me her little baby again.

"I didn't want you to get the wrong idea, love," Winks says, kissing her temple.

"I'll have to watch out for him, won't I half-man?" she says to me with a faint burp. She topples slightly on her heels. She blows a jet of air out the corner of her mouth to try and get a loose hair strand out of her eyes. "You're a better catch than I thought," she smiles blearily to Winks. "I can attract glances too, you know." She tugs on his tie and attempts a catwalk twirl but trips into his arms halfway through it. He hugs her with a tight jerk around her hips that tips her off balance. He pats her bottom. She lets out a yelp of pretend offence, so he pats her bottom again.

They walk hand in hand to the carpark in the centre of the course, him swinging his binoculars like a rubber walking-stick, her shoes spiking the ticker-tape of discarded betting slips. There's Uncle Chicka bending down and shouting, his shirt melted on his skin with sweat. He has gathered a dozen punters in a circle around him to play two-up. He wears his doctor's bag over his bull-nose belly, reaches into it for twenty-dollar notes. He smells them with a grand inhaling and slaps one down on the gravel like a challenge. Winks plays Snap with it with a twenty-dollar note of his own and yells out "Twenty the tails." The circle-men free their arms from the arms of their wives or girlies and peel twenties and tens from their rolls, hold the money high in the air for all to see, then pat the money to the ground. Other men play Snap on it: "Fifty the heads," they yell. "I'll take you on."

"Go the tails," Heels barracks, handing me twenty dollars to bet for her so she doesn't have to bend down and get unsteady. Uncle Chicka nods, acknowledging the bet as I Snap it into place in the dust. "How you going, Digger?" he says as he nods. He calls everyone Digger, even the women. "Man your position, Digger," he winks to me and makes a clicking with his tongue. "Go on look-out for coppers." I wink back, not sure if he really expects me to go on look-out, or if he's playing up to the crowd to sharpen their thrill of doing something illegal like playing two-up. I expect it's the latter and place my hand above my eyes like a visor, pretending to scour the landscape. "That's the boy," he belly-laughs. Other bellies and women's breasts, including Heels', join in.

"Oh he's a good lookout all right," she announces to everyone. "He's been keeping an eye on his old man all day. I've had a full report thank you very much."

Uncle Chicka places a twenty-cent coin with a yellow cross on it on his index finger, another crossed coin on his middle fingertip and calls out *Come in spinner*. He flicks the coins heavenward as if giving the world the fingers sign. The coins spin and tinkle across the pebbles. "Tails!"

THERE'S NO SUCH THING as punishment if you believe in God. There is forgiveness, a clean slate granted by God for repenting sins and believing in him. Yet Winks has not repented and his rubbing the girlies' hollows has brought no punishment, no yelling-talk, no tears. Instead, all Heels goes on about is a new car. We've bought a new car, a maroon car, just like the Heritage Mercedes we used to have. When I see it I'm under orders to remark to her and Winks that "Oh yes, it looks exactly like the Mercedes," because that's how she is going to consider it, a bit of a Mercedes called a Torana. Who wants a real Mercedes anyway when they cost such a fortune and the money is better spent in the business department at the moment, and the apartment department? Not to mention the right sort of school for his nibs.

And look over there at the man they call Perce Galea. There's no sign of repentance in him, and him an owner of Sydney's illegal gambling dens, a briber of politicians and police so the papers hint and my uncles say, though my uncles mean it as flattery.

Saturday. Dawn. I've driven with Winks in the Torana-

Mercedes to Randwick trackwork. Me to be near God's athletes as they gallop invisibly out there in the half-dark past the blank, empty grandstands. Him to stand, hand on hips, with other men and their hands on hips, sportscoats parted as if presenting their stomachs like a badge for important, private speaking. In the centre of the course, the place where cars park on race-day and Uncle Chicka flicks his crossed coins, there's a tin shed where trainers and owners lean out the windows and squint through binoculars into the grey-black morning. A caravan of horses circles the shed until the riders peel them off in ones, twos and threes and Tommy Smith orders them to "do three in thirty-six" or "six half pace, three evens" in the boy-jockey voice of an old racing man. He tilts from side to side, bandy-legged, when he walks and wears a suit, tie and panama hat because this racecourse is his office, he says. How else would you turn up for work in the morning in an office! For other trainers in their gumboots and jumpers and windcheaters this must be their farm, he cackles.

The word goes round: Perce Galea is coming. Here comes Perce Galea. Here's Mr Galea, the sportsjacket men say. "Good morning, Mr Galea," I say in the round of shaking hands. His black porkpie hat is tipped to one side on his head, his brown long-coat and suit coat are unbuttoned and billowing like a cloak. His tanned face is glittery with grey morning-stubble. This time of day, morning, is his evening. His dens are closed for this, his night. He's on his way home to bed but first he wants to pat his racehorse, to shake hands with the sportjackets, to part his coats and point his belly and ask, "What's the fucking story? Bit of a nip in the air." He says fuck and cunt two or three times a sentence and says them loudly and nobody hushes him. Winks says, "He never swears in front of women. He's a thorough gentleman in that regard."

I take every opportunity to stand next to Mr Galea, to think "I'm standing next to a crime boss, I'm an important person now, someone not to be trifled with." He tells me to piss off with a jerk of his head and a half-whistle, he wants to talk business with the sportsjackets. I don't go away so he gives me five dollars and says, Scram. When I refuse to accept the five dollars he gives a half-whistle to Winks to come here and explain what the fuck's wrong with his son who doesn't accept five fucking dollars.

"Don't be rude to Mr Galea. Take it," frowns Winks.

"A kid's too fucking spoilt who refuses five dollars. When I was a kid I'd of fucking killed for five dollars. Kids these days don't fucking know what it's like to be fucking poor." He appears to be reprimanding Winks but he's smiling and patting the side of my face kindly.

Winks follows his lead with a smile and a pat of his own on my back. "He's gone all religious at the moment, sorry Perce."

"Is that right? That's a fucking good thing." Mr Galea keeps patting me. "There's not enough of us religious in this fucking world." He says he never trusts any cunt who doesn't have a strong belief in God. He's been recommended for an honour from the Catholic Church, a Catholic knighthood approved by the Pope himself no less. Why? Because he dedicates every spare fucking moment to the Church. They want a new roof, they get a new fucking roof. They want damp coursing at the Cathedral, they get fucking damp coursing at the Cathedral. A man should go to church every chance he gets. Go to Mass. "You Catholic?" he pats.

"Church of England," I say proudly and so does Winks.

Mr Galea says it doesn't matter if I'm Catholic or not a Catholic, just as long as I go to church and pray. Because then if I die tomorrow, I'm fucking covered. OK? Yes? Good boy. He says to call him Uncle Perce from now on because I'm a good boy.

*

What does Winks do for a living apart from pointing his stomach with the sportsjacket men, peeling his roll to back a winner or loser? No hotel has been bought, no business, no apartment. The cabbage-smelling, wine-cask-smelling flat is now referred to as home where once Heels would call it the stopover. Is Winks unemployed? Is he gambling away the family savings? Stephen Papadopoulos's father is a grocer. "My dad's a grocer with his own shop," he boasts. Jonathan Jonathan's father is a taxi driver: "He works fourteen hours a day." Winks tells me he's looking for a business to buy, but no business is bought.

"That's what they all say," Stephen insists. "That's code for unemployed—'Waiting for the right business.' You must really be poor. Your father must be on the dole."

So demeaning to be thought of as really poor, with a father on the dole. I tell them my family is worth $200,000, and that it used to be $400,000. It's an admission that I'd lied to them, that I never did immigrate to Australia with nothing as Greeks and Arabs do, but I don't care now about being a liar. I prefer to have my pride than their friendship. They guffaw that they don't believe me and that it's no shame to be poor with a father on the dole.

"It's true, $400,000."

What are they sniggering at now, out of your earshot? Are they saying their fathers with their can't-speak-English English and wrong colour skin have done so well in life compared to mine?

"What are you talking about?" I plead them to tell. "What are you saying? I know you're saying something about me. Don't walk away from me. Come back."

They call to me that I should go be with Glenn Shivington. He's Anglo like me, they say. He's been following me around for weeks and trying to sit next to me in the classroom. Go be with Glenn Shivington even though he's a Sniff.

Is Glenn Shivington really a Sniff? He has to be a Sniff with his small girl-face and fleece-hair of yellow curls, his gold-wire spectacles, his gangly flinging arms and wrists when he walks or runs. He's smart too, the smartest boy in school. The playground girls, the girls who go shoeless at lunch to paint their toe ends, are certain of it—he's a Sniff, they complain, tucking their skirt hems into their underwear and splaying on the scorching concrete for the sun. They can smell it on him, they sneer. Girls know a Sniff when they see one. Sniffs are like them but are not one of them and that's enough somehow to make the girls angry.

I won't allow a Sniff to sit beside me in class. But he has to sit somewhere and eventually comes the day Mr Surridge points him to sit beside me because the seats, all of which are two-seaters, are taken except mine.

"What was the date of Australian Federation?" Mr Surridge nods for me to answer. I have no idea. Glenn Shivington whispers through spidery fingers, "1901."

"1901," I answer. Mr Surridge says that I am indeed correct. He strides slowly between the desks for another child to question. I reprimand Glenn that I didn't need his help and was going to answer 1901 anyway.

"No you weren't," Glenn pipes up. All this time, these weeks of him lingering and staring shyly at me, he's never said a word. Now he's not only speaking to me he's contradicting me in a rapid, excited whisper. "You couldn't answer it by yourself. If you can answer by yourself then answer this: Who is the Prime Minister of Australia?"

"Leave me alone." I don't know who the Prime Minister of Australia is. "I haven't lived here that long," is the excuse I give.

"In what year did Captain Cook discover Australia?"

If we weren't in class, if we were out in the concrete paddock with its jungle bars and cricket nets I'd shove him hard to shut him up. But because I'm trapped into listening to him like this, silence is my only defence. Yet he prods his way through it with "Don't you want to do well in the exams?"

"I've been reading the bible a lot. I'll start studying tonight."

"You only have a month. I don't think you're smart enough to learn everything in a month."

"Who cares."

"You won't get into Sydney High."

"Who cares. I'll go to a private school."

"No you won't. Your father doesn't even have a job. You can't afford a private school."

"We *can*."

Glenn Shivington sits quietly a moment then says he believes me. If I say we can afford it then he has no evidence, no reason not to believe me, it's the obvious scientific deduction he must draw. Being able to afford a private school would certainly explain my being lazy and not studying or caring, he goes on.

But he cares, he says. He cares that I won't be going to Sydney High because he'll be going there he's sure and he wishes I were too, that we could both be going there together.

"Why?"

"I'd just like it. Why don't you let me help you study?" He reels off that the Prime Minister of Australia is Gough Whitlam, James Cook discovered Australia in 1770. Then there's Lachlan Macquarie, a very important name for exams. He was Governor of New South Wales from 1810 till 1821 and is sometimes referred to as the father of the nation.

Glenn Shivington can recite geography facts from capital cities to weather patterns and rain catchment figures. He can multiply fractions and solve long division in his head. He stares at me when he speaks. I can sense him examining my face. "What are you staring at," I challenge him. He blushes and says "Nothing" and begins staring again. I sit at the very end of my seat as far away from him as I can to demonstrate my aversion to Sniffs to the rest of the class in case they're looking.

Later in the day, just as we're about to enter class for the maths session, he touches my elbow then quickly holds up his hands in defence as if expecting me to strike him. I pull my elbow away from him and turn my back. "Can I sit beside you?" he asks meekly. I don't answer but once we're in the classroom I do something inexplicable—I catch his eye and put my hand on the seat beside me to signal he can sit there if he wants. Surely it's because I realise he can be useful to me with his facts and fractions. It can't be because I enjoy his whispering and staring.

When he leans across to provide the answer for 6820 divided by 43, taking the opportunity to explain how 68.2 can be expressed as a percentage of 6820, and the whole confounding logic of decimals is actually very easy, his breath grazes my cheek, my neck. When his shoulder presses against my shoulder I allow the pressing to go on for a few seconds before I nudge him away to put some distance between us. I refuse to say thanks for his scribbled explanations and diagrams to make the distance even greater, yet that only makes him breathe even closer next time, press more determinedly. On one occasion he attempts his pressing without any school reason, no maths to solve, no spelling of a tricky word like *entrepreneur*. I bump him up to sit straight and insist he keep to his side of the desk unless I give him permission, the signal for which is my asking him for help. He apologises in a faint, hurt mutter then summons enough courage to tell me he predicts I'll fail the exams.

"Then what's the point of me sitting next to you?" I say. "What use are you?"

He's muttering again, faintly, head in hands. "I don't want to go to Sydney High by myself. I don't want to go without you."

I tell him that it will be his fault if I don't go to Sydney High. If he were any kind of friend at all he would make sure he helped me answer the questions *in* the exams. That's the time I really need the answers—in the actual exam, not now. He should organise himself to help me answer the questions *during* the exam. If the exam desks are two-seaters he should sit beside me and show me his answers. If the desks are one-seaters he should sit in front of me and pretend to lean back and stretch regularly, letting me glimpse his answer sheet in the process.

Glenn makes no reply. It's as if he hasn't been listening. When, after a minute or so, he leans across to speak it's only to point out that the latest entry in my exercise book is wrong: if a ceiling is 283 centimetres above a floor and a table is 77 centimetres and the bookcase on top of the table is 197 centimetres high then a 9 centimetre space is left, not 19 as I've written. I poke at him to sit up straight and stop pressing on me. When he tries to lurch closer to me I jab him. For the next few days I jab and poke him to mind his own business. Finally he lurches across and says "I want to tell you something" and begs me not to keep forcing him to stay away. "I'll show you the answers during the exam." He presses against my shoulder as if helping with my schoolwork though there is no schoolwork to do. I let him press and breathe. It's not entirely unpleasant the warm feel of our shoulders touching. His breath doesn't smell—there's no Stephen garlic smell. No sign of fear at what we are planning, no guilt or shame. He must believe in God. He, the brightest boy in school, will have realised long ago that there's no such thing as punishment if you believe in God.

BETTING TICKETS COVER RANDWICK like paper snow. It must be kicked aside just to walk to the bookmakers' rails or the mesh gate where whitecoats demand to see your Members badge before letting you through.

"What are the chances of one of those tickets still being alive," rasps Uncle Chicka placing his arm around my shoulder to share some information. "What's the chance some poor bugger accidentally threw away a live ticket and you picked it up?"

I shrug that one in a million might be a close figure. Uncle Chicka pokes the air in front of my chest with his middle finger and grins at Winks who is finding Chicka's line of questioning intriguing. Winks has clasped his hands behind his back, playing at standing to attention before a teacher. Uncle Chicka estimates the chances would be far better than a million to one. "I'd agree with you," Winks interrupts, causing Uncle Chicka to hold up a hand, close his eyes and hush Winks like a father would.

Uncle Chicka asks me to put a number on how many people do I think would be here at the races today. When I shake my head against venturing a guess he makes me take a stab at a figure. I offhandedly suggest ten thousand and he agrees that that would be about right or close enough to it. He poses this question: if there are ten thousand people here today and each person has a single bet in each race and one or other mug out of that ten thousand accidentally discards a winning ticket, and this happens every race and we're up to Race Four now, and I got out there in the crowd, down on my hands and knees and checked, say, four tickets a minute, how many tickets would I have to sort through before I found a winning ticket?

Glenn Shivington would answer this in a flash but I can merely chew my lip ignorantly. Uncle Chicka has to relieve me of having to provide an answer. "What I'm saying is," he says, "you should take this result sheet (he hands me a list of the day's place-getting horses) and update it with the first three horses of each race and get out there and start scouring through tickets. Because I tell you this my boy, there could be a bloody fortune waiting for you under all those feet. And that should keep you occupied and let your father enjoy himself at the races in peace."

So what if there's a fortune waiting for me, what would I do with it? I'm twelve going on thirteen in two, three, four months. Heels and Winks would take the money off me. They'd take it for themselves and say they have every right to do so because look at what it costs to keep me in shoes with my big feet always growing and clothes that can only be let down so many times. And food—steaks don't grow on trees in case I haven't noticed. Now private schools, that will put one hell of a dent in the budget. Yes, I should be a bit more grateful and put my new-found fortune into the family kitty instead of being so selfish. If I'm like this at twelve what on earth will I be like at thirty!

What if I don't tell them about it, where would I hide the money? The stopover flat has no crannies behind brick for a hiding place, no floorboards or panels easily budged. The thing to do would be this: go to one of the wizened child-men, or all of them—it depends on the size of the fortune. Say, "Here's X amount of dollars to stop whipping and spurring God's athletes." There's no likelihood of stopping them otherwise. Winks says I'm being silly about the child-men. Face up to it, he tells me: these people are making a living and have to hit the horses or else they get into trouble by the authorities for not trying to win the race. That's the rules. Besides, horses don't feel it, he says. They're just horses, they're stupid and don't feel pain. "When did you ever hear a horse cry out in pain? Never."

Not cry out but squeal, I'm about to say. Squeal and snort when he himself and Charlie Carmichael thrashed them with the clipper cord. But Winks talks over the top of me. "I want you to stop following me around and asking me to go bother jockeys with your ridiculous notions. There are things in this world you can't prevent and the whipping and spurring of racehorses is one of them."

Money. That's what the child-men understand and that's what I'll give them. Out through the first snow-covering of tickets I go, out among the trouser cuffs of the Members with their perfectly straight blade-creases. Tan slip-on shoes with tassels, and black shiny lace-ups. For an hour I crouch and search and fail. I move on, out through the next much thicker covering of tickets—long brown bookie cards and totalisator stubs. Here the slip-ons are blue canvas or rubber thongs with yellow toenails. Scuffed brown brogues that have odd-coloured laces. The heaped tickets are slippery as moss where I step, and when I plunge my hands into them they run through my fingers like paper water.

Tote ticket: Race Three, number seven, ten dollars each way; a loser—a deadie. Race Three, number four, five dollars the win; dead. Race Three, bookie's ticket, number four, twenty dollars a win is what I think the bookie squiggle reads; dead. Race Two, number one, Masquraider, a squiggled twenty dollars to win; dead. All dead. The more futile the task seems the more certain I am the next ticket will be live. I pray, Please God provide justice in the next ticket, for your animal athletes whose chestnuts you made with your hammer.

"No joy there, Periscope?" Tennis shoes, tracksuit pants with Adidas three-stripe. "We call you Periscope with your up-down, up-down looking for tickets."

This man who is speaking to me has the faded blue handwriting of hori tattoos on his knuckles and wrists—*Rita, Legman, mum, hate.* But this man is no hori, though he's frightening all the same. His pakeha forearms are orange with freckles and decorated in the snake and nude women of a pakeha. A front tooth is missing. His long oily hair falls in Cs and Ss onto his shoulders. His mouth has a ginger horseshoe round it for a beard.

"Listen Periscope," he says crouching and crawling forward to be closer to me. I flinch away. "I'm not going to hurt you, Periscope. I need a favour. Do a fella a favour? For ten dollars? That's more than you'll get scrounging about on the ground."

He tells me to answer Yes or No immediately. Yes or No,

quick, there's not time to fuck about, he says. Yes or no? But even before I can ask what sort of favour he wants me to do he says he's had an eye on me all day and I'm the kind of clean-cut boy a man can trust, decked out nicely in my sports-jacket like a little gentleman. No other cunt around here's worth pissing on but I've got honesty written all over my face. He bets I've been brought up proper.

All he wants me to do is take his Crops—he draws from his tracksuit pockets a black wallet, conceals it in his fist and slips it into my inside coat pocket; then another black wallet; then a brown one and a gold money clip with money folded into it like an ironed handkerchief. And take his Tin—two silver-coloured watches, a gold bracelet which he drops into my coat's side pockets. Take them and get up and walk out of the betting ring, right out through the gates and off the race-course altogether, then up Alison Road until I get to Cowper Street, and keep going up Cowper Street until I reach Avoca Street. From there cross into Avoca Street and keep going until I see an old green Zephyr. That's his car. When I get to that car I'm to wait till he comes and meets me—a half-hour, an hour at the most—and collects his Crops and Tin and puts ten dollars in my kick. "OK Periscope? Don't let me down. You'll notice I'm trusting you. Not threatening you. Shake. Shake." He shakes my hand. I shake in return. He has a wide, limp, clammy hand-squeeze. "I've picked the right man. See you, Periscope." He glances this way, that way, all over the place. Then he's gone through the slalom of the crowd.

I've never seen this person before yet he has given me a nickname and asked me for a favour to do with wallets that for some reason he calls Crops that now hang heavy against my ribs, watches and bracelets he calls Tin against my hips.

I finger inside my pockets to the smooth leather, imagining the notes of money there that I could open up like a book and thumb like pages. The watch metal feels cool as wetness. Should I take it all out of my pockets and inspect it? What if I dropped the money clip and the money blew away or was snatched from me, stolen? If I arrive at Avoca Street with money missing or if I don't arrive at all but take what's in my pockets home and keep it, what happens? The ginger man shook my hand like a friend and offered me a ten-dollar reward.

Ten dollars is not enough money for any of the child-men. What one of them would ever stop whipping and spurring for such a tiny sum! Everybody knows, every uncle I now have is always saying it can take hundreds to make a child-man pull up a horse for a bookie. But ten dollars will be a start, the first ten dollars saved. The problem remains: where can I keep my ten dollars? How do I stop Heels saying, "I'll take that, thank you very much. Consider it room and board"?

*

The entrance and exit of the course are not guarded as usual by whitecoats old and fat and dozing on stools at this time of the day but by blueshirts—a row of police blocking each wood archway or pacing with pistol handles sticking out from their belts like an ear. Four blueshirts have surrounded a man. They shove their fingers into his jean pockets with such force his bum-crack is exposed. He's wearing only a T-shirt shape of brown arms and white body because a blueshirt is shaking out his T-shirt like a table cloth and turning it inside-out. Another blueshirt peers inside the man's mouth, another is pulling apart the man's newspaper form-guide and jiggling each page as if expecting something to drop. They tell the man to sit on the grass and remove his shoes and socks. They flick and shake these as if to remove a stone or some sand. When nothing falls out they toss his shoes and socks into his lap. I slow my walk to watch but one of the blocking and pacing blueshirts tells me not to waste my time lollygagging and looking at scum like that and waves me through the exit to have me get on my way.

Up Alison Road, the ginger man said. Up Alison Road and keep going to Cowper Street. Keep going and cross into Avoca Street. Keep going along this chain of parked cars looking for a green Zephyr. There's one. This must be it. Green with a few dings, a heat-ripple aura from the sun. Yes, this must be it. Nothing to do now but wait as instructed. I cross the street to a patch of tree shade and sit in it on the warm concrete. To pass time I build a leaf-dam to block ants from going about their business en route to a hole in the footpath.

The ginger man is jog-walking up the street towards me. With him is a man almost his spitting image—his brother?—same body shape, face lines, complexion, though his hair is shorter, his tracksuit pants red not blue, and now that he's closer I see his hand tattoos are of spider-webs and a blue skull rather than rough handwriting. My chest thumps. Fear. Even though the ginger man calls me his little mate and smiles, puffing slightly, he snaps his fingers for me to obey him and give him his things, quick, quick, snap, snap, "Give it to me here."

I tremble and fumble to present the wallets as fast as he demands. I almost drop the watches from my cupped palm. The spitting image man glances about worriedly. Ginger man passes him the watches and bracelet and he acknowledges they are Nice Tin. Ginger man opens the wallets, pinches the brown-green edges of the bills and plucks them into his tracksuit pocket, saying that he's very grateful to me for my help because things got very hot there suddenly for him and he doesn't mean the weather. He had to do a dump and run. But everything's fine now thanks to me. He flips through the wallets' Diners Club cards, a photo of some children, a driver's licence. He pockets the driver's licence and Diners. "Here's your ten dollars. See you Periscope," he says stretching over a brick garden wall in front of a block of flats and dropping the wallets into a rubbish bin there. He puts his finger to his lips. "Mum's the word? Ay?" He unlocks the Zephyr's driver door and hops in, reaching over to pop up the lock for the spitting image man. They both wince at sitting on burning upholstery. Ginger man has to use his handkerchief to grip the wheel and steer away.

*

It's the talk of the Members Bar. Police are warning patrons to beware of pickpockets. The loudspeaker suspects three teams have been active on-course today.

Women inspect their handbags, purses. Men put down their beer glasses and dig in their pockets: left and right trouser, inside and outside coat. They compete to speak as experts on the subject of pickpockets: how the bastards will be professionals, professionals can slice open a hip-pocket like so with a blade cutter—the wallets just drop into their hands like fruit. The audacity of them! They snip off watches as easy as cutting string. They have no trouble with handbags, they unsnib them and take a lucky dip inside without you feeling a thing. "Isn't that right, Frank?" they call out to the racecourse detective who is nudging through the smoke-shrouded bar two steps this way, two steps that like a distracted dance. He removes his porkpie for the women and asks, unsmilingly, if anyone wishes to report possessions missing. He glances at his fob watch impatiently and tips it back into his waistcoat.

"What's this mob's go, Frank?" they ask firmly as if his superiors. "What's the story?"

The story, he tells them, is that this mob appears to be a gang from the Western Suburbs. They work a classic Fly, Gloves, Legman routine: the Fly chooses his Joe, moves in against the flow of people, bumps into him, in-out with his hand, passes the wallet to a Glove who catches it in his newspaper like a softball mitt and in turn passes it to a Legman who bolts as quick as a hare.

"Caught anyone, Frank?"

"We're working on it," he replies coolly.

Winks stands beneath the race replay television. He's telling a girlie that he keeps his spondulicks *here* in his side pockets. He produces a wad of cash from his right pocket then stuffs it deep down against his thigh. You can't feel a thief's hand go into your hip-pocket, sweetie. You can't feel it go inside your coat or your jacket. But you can always feel a hand go down here. "It's a very sensitive part of the body," he winks to her. "It's like an alarm. Go on. Try. Try and take my money without me feeling it."

He begins walking on the spot as if taking a casual stroll. The girlie slowly slips her hand into his pocket, grimacing with carefulness. He keeps strolling on the spot and doesn't react until she has delved to a depth where the cash would be and he can't stand the tickling sensation any longer and bursts out laughing, clasping his hands over the bulge of her hand. She pulls his money out and playfully waves it under his nose, not allowing him to grab it away. When finally he does snatch it he kisses her on the cheek in the same rapid movement.

"Isn't that right, Frank? Keep your money in your side pocket?" he asserts more than asks.

"If you say so Sir," the detective replies. "All your possessions accounted for?"

The girlie puts her fingers up to her mouth in mock panic. "I'm short twenty dollars. Will the police reimburse me?"

"The last race is where that twenty dollars went," says Winks, laughing and holding her closer by her hollow.

The detective pinches his hat brim politely and moves on.

*

I own ten dollars. The first money I've ever earned. But it's stolen money. Perhaps it was from someone right here in the Members: from that handbag, in that pocket. Winks' pockets even. It serves them right. It serves Winks right too for not paying attention to God's athletes except as odds and form and weights to be carried, too busy with beers and hollows to be bothered with the child-men dealing out beatings. This ten dollars is God's money. It's for his use, and that makes the stealing right. It makes justice.

I wait for the ginger man the following Saturday. He doesn't appear. I wait the Saturday after that, though that Saturday is a Rosehill race-day. And so is the one after that. I wait and wait at Rosehill and Randwick. I'm here, I mutter to the air, to nobody. "It's me, Periscope. It's Periscope." At home I'm the first to be dressed for the races instead of a sulky dawdler. "He's caught the bug," Heels says. "Isn't it nice that we've found something we can do as a family?" I search for the green, dinged Zephyr in Alison Road, in Cowper and Avoca streets.

The next Saturday when the races are at Warwick Farm and Heels and Winks decide to take the train because Warwick Farm is in the "woop woop", I go there too and take up position among the yellow toenails and scuffed minglers, the slippery river of paper. But the ginger man doesn't come. I never see him again. I cellotape the ten dollars to the back of my bedhead. I've imagined many tens of dollars that would be added by helping the ginger man sneak his pickings off course. I can't understand why praying hasn't brought him to me. I'd be angry at God but what a notion—to be angry at God. Who dares be angry at God? If this is another test of me, what test could that be? A test of patience?

Could it be a test of resourcefulness? If so, could it be that I'm supposed to become a pickpocket to help his athletes by myself? I have no accomplices. The racecourse detective spoke of a Gloves with a newspaper, a Legman, a Fly. Am I meant to work alone? I begin to observe where people keep their wallets. There are hip-pocket people, there are inside-pocket people. There are no-wallet men whose cash is crumpled and needs to be teased out so they don't spill their change. There are women whose handbags gape and swing like binoculars. There are women who keep their handbags clipped tight to be carried under their arms like rugby balls.

At home I begin to practise my moves. It is Sunday. Heels and Winks will be gone for the afternoon. They say they're inspecting a business to buy. There is also an apartment they think is worth a look. I'm not to leave the flat. I'm to amuse myself in some way, which shouldn't be too hard surely. And don't open the door to strangers.

Winks' wardrobe slides across. His smells stir, swirl onto me—his citrus Q-Tol aftershave, his creamy Brylcreem and hardly detectable whiff of BO. His suits hang side-on like people queuing—two blue pin-stripe, one shiny copper-brown, two dark grey, two shingle grey. I part the queue, choose the copper one for practice. I slip my right hand through the front, pretending to barge open the jacket in a mash of race-day bodies. I measure my success by how little the jacket swings on the rail. In my mind this equates to how heavy or light my touch is, how easily noticed by a victim. Speed is also important. My hand must be in-out of a pocket in an instant. This works best, I discover, when my hand is perfectly flat as a karate chop.

It's going to take a lot of practice for the suits not to swing. Perhaps more practice than I have the patience for. My left hand is the steadier. It's my natural hand, stronger, nimbler, the hand I use to throw a ball or hold a bat. My right hand might be my writing hand, but that's only because of a piece of string. My left hand is my real hand.

After an hour's practice I've moved along the line of suits, my fingers tonging from the pockets a handkerchief, a three-week-old race book. And a fifty-dollar note. Those new fifty dollars the government brought out. I decide to cellotape it to the back of my bedhead with the ten dollars. Then I decide against that. Then for it. Is it theft to take this fifty dollars from my own father? I wouldn't want to thieve from my own father. But he is my father and therefore it can't be theft. Theft is taking from people you don't know. I will tape the money to my bedhead, theft or no theft. Let this be the way my father helps God's athletes.

On Heels' side of the wardrobe which takes up three quarters of the whole space, dozens of pink and gold, blue and floral dresses and gowns hang like a bunched curtain. On the ledge above, three pyramids of hat boxes—brimmed hats on the bottom, brimless in the smaller boxes on top. Each hat crammed with tissue paper. They are hats which themselves wear hats of plastic to protect their stiff veils and rose posies of cloth. At one end of the rack, zipped in its own transparent raincoat, Heels' mink coat the colour of a dirty cloud. The colour she calls sable. Hardly ever worn, but "that's not the point," she says. "It's very expensive and nice to say you own one."

Her shoes of three shades—black, tan, fawn—stand at attention in rows. Along the wardrobe's back wall, black, tan, fawn handbags to match them. Some stuffed with tissue paper; others contain a sediment of loose change she calls *chicken-feed* and hairpins, an eyebrow pencil, peppermints, peppermint foil, a face-powder puff. I balance a bag on the edge of the bathroom vanity and practise flicking apart the two metal fingers that snib it shut. When, half an hour later, that can be done without the bag toppling to the floor I practise unsnibbing it and dipping my hand, my karate chop, inside in the same movement. When that can be done—it takes no more than twenty minutes—I open the wardrobe drawers. Winks' side, top drawer: clothes brush with tiny holsters for nail clippers, a comb, tweezers, a tub of Brylcreem, cuff links, spare watch, stopwatch, arm braces, tie pin. Heels' side, top drawer: jewellery box, headscarves with Cleopatra patterns, sunglasses, evening gloves. The jewellery box is laden with tangled treasure: bracelets, pearls, rings with amber, diamond and purple stones, clip-on earrings like metal rocks that I attach to my earlobes, stretching them painfully.

I drip chains and pearls into a handbag to practise snatching them back. When bored with that I try on the pearls, the necklaces with diamond or red insets. I try on rings with blue glass, gold bracelets with heart-shaped locks, silk headscarves that wrap up my big ears and hair, Chinesing my eyes. I have become a boy-woman: chest hairless and smooth, its muscles forming like flat breasts, nipples brown as two-cent pieces, hardening cold and tingling if I rub them.

Upon Heels' drawers there is a makeup case which opens like a palette, an artist's box of lipsticks, eye shadows, creams, powders and scent bottles. I dab and gloss myself with red lips and cheeks, blue-black eyes, eyebrows perfectly arched as brown moustaches. I remove the mink coat's cover, taking great care not to catch the fur in the cover's zipper. It is softer than anything I have ever stroked, this fur. Not even horse skin is so soft, or my own skin, my cocko's wrinkled peel. The coat is wispy soft as dandelion which must be why she or anyone else would own such clothing: as a spare skin softer than human.

What other skins do they keep here? I have the back of my bedhead for secrets. What do *they* have? Winks' drawer third one down: neatly folded handkerchiefs, cravats and scarves, two wallets with a poor man's lock of rubber bands which I remove—his birth certificate, marriage certificate, brittle and creased. Paper bundles: bank statements—"$1000" written at the bottom of one page, "$600" on another.

Heels' drawer, third one down: bottles of doctor's pills with *take two after meals* on the label, Bex, Disprin. Her fourth drawer down, the deepest: two spare sets of teeth, Dr Scholls corn pads, ointment for cracked soles, a deodorant spray called Femme Fresh, two little cushions curved like so in the shape of breasts. Winks' last drawer down: balls of socks, white Y-fronts, stacks of handkerchiefs still in cellophane boxes.

In movies, walls and drawers have sliding panels and hidden safes, false bottoms for code books and rare stones, briefcases full of millions in United States currency to be given in exchange for information. I tap and knock, though Heels and Winks aren't spies or Sean Connery. There are no secret compartments except layers of socks and smalls. Beneath them a magazine with foreign writing. "Danish" is the only word I can understand. But this isn't a magazine of words. This is a magazine whose first page is a photograph of two women and two men walking into a living room. Whose second page is one of the men putting his hand under a woman's skirt, the other man putting his hand down her top which the second woman is unbuttoning. The second woman's own blouse is unbuttoned, one of her breasts is exposed. On the third page these people have taken off their clothes and are sticking out the tips of their tongues and kissing with them. The two men's cockos are swelled like little arms and fists. It is a magazine of legs and swelled cocko-arms, breasts, tongues, fingers and women's privates, their cunts. One cocko is halfway in one woman's mouth and the other cocko is in her cunt while the other woman is licking the tip of her tongue at the top of that cunt above where the cocko is, just at the place where the cunt-hair starts in a V pattern.

I've heard boys speak of such magazines belonging to older brothers and cousins. They are thrilling taboo things that shouldn't belong to a father, my Winks. What is a magazine doing here? I will ask him. But I can't ask him. He then would know I have been going through his private things. He disgusts me. I want to believe the magazine was here when we arrived in this flat, the shame of a former tenant. Winks has simply not yet disposed of it. He has forgotten about it altogether. Surely that's it.

Inside my cocko there is an itch, a pleasure-pain. My cocko is moving and bending against my underpants. Its skin-sack has sucked up into itself, tight and filling up with the itch that's inside my cocko. I've forgotten to breathe. My heart thuds as if I have just sprinted a long distance. I'm paralysed by what's happening in my cocko—it has now swelled as in the photographs in the magazine. The itching and pleasure-pain has spread deep inside my belly, has paralysed and terrified me. It has taken control of me—the slightest movement makes the swelling feel worse, feel better. I drop the magazine into the drawer and kick it closed to will the itching and stiffening to stop. To shut the fucking and mouthing people out of my mind.

The telephone is ringing in the lounge. My legs are so weak and trembly they cannot make a stride, but I must answer it. If I don't answer it and it is Heels and Winks they'll wonder why the phone is ringing out. They'll rush home and there I'll be with my cocko swollen, my head too addled to hurry the makeup from my face and put everything back as I found it.

"Hello," I try to answer brightly. It's Heels. She wants to know if everything is all right at home. Yes, I answer. What am I doing? she asks. Watching TV? Yes. She says they quite like the business they've seen. They're excited in fact. They want to sit down with a cup of tea somewhere nice and discuss the proposition. They'll be home in a short while. Have some ham from the fridge to make a sandwich if I'm hungry.

The sweet pain, the itching, shaking and stiffness have eased. The fucking and mouthing people keep flashing before my mind's eye but I turn my mind's eye the other way by concentrating on washing the makeup from my real eyes and my lips, using a nail brush and soap to scrub until my lips taste of the metallic tang of blood. I hang the handbag on its hook, fold the headscarf away, return the jewellery. I sweat so much I wish I could shower but I mustn't see my body naked like the fucking and mouthing people. I mustn't see my cocko or touch it even though I want to touch it and want to let my mind's eye glimpse the remembered photographs. I want my real eyes to look at the real photographs once again. I must somehow let the magazine lie at the bottom of the drawer and cover it with socks and handkerchiefs, and I must do it with my mind's eye and my real eyes closed.

I NVITE A NICE FRIEND TO STAY the night by all means. What a good idea if I'm studying for exams. But Glenn Shivington says he cannot accept the invitation. He has polio, or is in danger of getting polio, it isn't entirely clear which. He sleeps with his legs in braces, his ankles are manacled to the bed-end. He isn't allowed to sleep at my place or anyone else's for that matter because he can't spend a night away from his braces and manacles, and what an effort it would be to transport them anywhere. I will have to stay at his place instead.

Polio? Can you catch polio from him? Heels wonders. "I don't want you around people with polio. Should a child in that condition even be at school spreading disease?" She'll have to make enquiries. She doesn't like this polio business one bit. She'll have a cigarette on it. She'll pour a glass from the cask and have a sit-down with a cigarette and ponder this one and ring the doctor. Mind you, what do doctors know, she mutters. Have they fixed her varicose veins? Look at them. They'll get where they'll show even through dark stockings.

Yes you can go to Glenn Shivington's because you've had the whatever-they-call-it that stops it, says the doctor. But go on one condition: that you come here to your mother and give her a big kiss for being such a good mother and protecting you from polio. There's the boy.

There are rules about being at Glenn Shivington's house which isn't a house but a flat in a Randwick khaki block like our stopover home but darker because it's close up against another khaki block and its windows cannot get the sun, and even if they did the blinds are kept closed always. His father lives in a wheelchair because of polio. I try not to stare at his legs, which are hardly like legs at all but empty trousers bent up from his footrests. Sometimes he can become very angry, Glenn says. He yells for no reason and throws books against the walls. But mostly he stays in his study and reads because he used to be a teacher. Glenn's mother when she talks, whispers to make less noise and not disturb his reading. I stay in Glenn's room playing Monopoly and nattering, not studying one iota except practising to sit behind him during exams, reading over his shoulder or glimpsing his answers if sitting side by side.

Has he ever gone through his parent's things? Has he ever had a peep at what's under their socks and smalls. No never, Glenn replies. "What chance would I have? My father never leaves the flat except to go to the doctor." What does he think he'd find if he did look? He doesn't know. He's never considered it. I've looked beneath my parent's socks and smalls, I tell him. There was a magazine full of fucking and mouthing people. I even put on my mother's makeup and mink coat and wrapped a scarf into a turban and paraded in her mirror. Hasn't he ever done that? No. He asks what it's like to put on makeup. He watches his mother put her face on but she won't let him touch her things. She says it's not for boys, and besides, she has no jewellery except a wedding ring which she only removes for the dishes. He hates being a boy. I ask him if he's really a Sniff. *No*, he says like a protest and points at me that if I want to wear makeup then I must be a Sniff myself. But I only wore makeup for something to do, I protest back. Just like when I practised pickpocketing—it was something to do. I'm not a Sniff. Glenn says he doesn't know what he is. He doesn't believe for one minute that I'm a pickpocket or have ever known pickpockets, but if I put on makeup then that's the behaviour of a Sniff. He's sniggering how he wouldn't like to see me in makeup because he imagines I'd look ugly with my blunt, chubby features. He'd prefer to look at me as the real boy I am, not as some girl-boy.

He wants to know if I might be able to steal some makeup from Heels for him. I could consider it part of the cheating agreement between us. He makes me promise I will—just an eyeliner and lipstick will do. I shake on it, my squeezing mangrip against his thin, loose fingers.

I'll sleep tonight on an inflated lilo on the floor beside Glenn's iron-framed bed. His leg braces are screwed to the bed-end like steel chains with steel splints reaching up to his knees. Leather straps bind the splints in place. He must sleep on his back because his feet are locked in such a way that they can only point upwards. He says there's not much pain in lying this way though the steel sometimes creates a stretching sensation and makes him dream of walking on stilts a mile above other people, stilts that break and he falls but never hits the ground.

His mother calls him a brave boy and kisses his toes as she ties and clips him into bed like a prisoner for the night. The lights go off. There is static in my eyes from the sudden dark: the room returns to view dimly.

"Tell me what you saw," Glenn says.

"Saw where?"

"The magazines. The magazines."

What he wants are descriptions of the fucking and mouthing people. What do they look like with no clothes, with cocks (not cocko: cocko is a child's word, he says), cocks and cunts showing? Is it like when you stand in the mirror or look down in your underpants and your cock's gone stiff? Yes, it's like that, I say, but their cocks are much bigger with veins everywhere and hair.

"How many stiffies have you ever had?" he asks. I've had a few stiffies, I say, but not many. He wants to know when I have them. Waking up? He has them when he wakes up in the morning, he says. Same here, I say. But the ones I've been having recently are different from the stiffies I've had before. The other ones before just went away after a while. I'd wait a few seconds over the toilet bowl for my cock to be soft enough to piss and it went soft. But the new ones over the past month are different. How are they different? he wants to know. Is it that the stiffies stay stiff and your balls ache and make you feel sick? That's what they're like for him. Same here, I say.

He asks if I've ever woken up and it's all wet—my stomach, my pyjamas—like a half-piss. I don't want to answer that and instead ask, Have you? He replies, Yes, and then I say, Same here. His pyjamas dry hard as cardboard. Same here. And it's salty and smells like paint and detergent. He's sure he knows in his sleep exactly the moment the wet spurts out of him because he can feel himself waking up, but he doesn't quite wake up, doesn't *want* to wake up at that moment. He likes to lay there with his insides tickling and dream of touching his cock and of someone else touching his cock and him doing it to them, touching them, until his cock pulses and spurts in his dreams exactly at the same time as he's waking up in the wet in real life. He's started keeping his handkerchief under his pillow to wipe it up. He's found that if he unmanacles himself and gets out of bed straightaway after he's wiped himself up and washes the wet off with water the handkerchief doesn't go like cardboard. But getting to the bathroom without trailing the detergent smell behind him or letting the wet drip onto the carpet and leaving a cardboard patch is the problem. He finds it best to let it dry while still in bed and roll his pyjamas and handkerchief up and place it down the bottom of the washing basket for his mother. But that's happening every morning now. His mother must know something is wrong.

He asks me, "Do you ever bring it on yourself?" He means by rubbing my cock.

"No."

"Bullshit."

"Do you?"

"Once. Twice."

"Really?"

"Lots of times."

Sometimes he feels so itchy inside himself that he has to run into the toilet and rub himself till he empties out. Sometimes he does it straight into his handkerchief. "Don't you?"

"I've just started." I started a few weeks ago but stopped for fear of wasting away. Everyone would know what I'm doing if they saw I was wasting away. No matter how I itch and desperately want the itch and pulsing to go on and on, I don't rub my cock.

"I'm not wasting away," says Glenn. "Who told you you waste away?"

I don't know, I've just heard it said. Perhaps it was Winks who said it to someone and I overheard.

Glenn itches so much he was on a bus once, he says, and his cock went stiff and he couldn't help it and his pants stuck out so far with the shape of his cock that he had to put his school bag over the problem to get off the bus. Same here. But the bag rubbed against it and made the stiffie worse. He had to let the wet go into his pants while he was sitting there with the bus making the feeling worse-better at every bump. Same here. He's had to walk down the street with his bag over his crotch to cover the wet spot. Same here. He's sure the hot weather and a rocking bus always make him stiff. The hot weather makes his cock looser and warmer. Same here. His trick before getting on a bus is to rub himself and spurt out a good load into the toilet at home to stop him getting excited on the trip.

Every time I rub my cock I pray an apology to God. But Glenn doesn't believe God exists. His father can't understand how on earth a God that is supposed to be loving and decent would give anyone polio. "Do you know the answer to that?" Glenn asks me.

"No."

"God probably does it too, rubs his cock."

"You can't say that."

"God's probably rubbing his cock so much he's too wasted away to bother about polio and do any good in the world."

How can he utter such mockeries of God and not suffer a punishment either from the heavens or within his own body, a great pain or seizure tuned to respond automatically to God-mocking words or thoughts?

Glenn then asks if I'm stiff now this second. I answer No but he sits up in his bed and peers at my silhouette. I lift up my knees to cover my stiffie. He confesses that he's stiff—it's all this cock talk. I can look at his cock if I like, he says. No, I say, I don't want to, though I would like to compare his cock's shape to mine, its size, degree of hardness. To cross into another person's privacy of genitals. He asks if he can look at me, my stiff cock.

No.

I can hear the quick chafing of him rubbing his cock and pausing. Rubbing and pausing.

"Look at this." His voice is unsteady from his rubbing motion.

I sit up and crane for a glimpse. His cock points towards his stomach like a long finger. I lie back down and rub my own cock.

"Are you doing it?" he asks out of breath.

"Yes."

He sits up. My feet trample my sheet and blanket down so he can see me.

I stand beside his bed. We watch each other rubbing. His hand reaches out to take my cock in his fingers, lightly, tentative, as if stroking an animal for the first time. This action doesn't shock me, it's the obvious, the right action for that moment. I bend down and touch his cock, grip it, rub it. It's skinnier than mine. Narrower at the top. Its bow in the middle is more pronounced. An electric throb moves through my insides because here are fingers that are not my own, skin that is not my skin touching me down there, exploring the private ridge and the stem as if molding a shape from plasticine.

He gasps. His leg-braces chink on the bed-end from a spasm. A splash heavy as a summer rain-drop lands on the back of my hand and wrist. I stop rubbing to feel his cock pulse the wet out of him.

Now me—an itch and chill from the soles of my feet to my scalp, a shivering. I hear plops on the carpet. My limbs are suddenly weak.

Glenn's slimy wet is already drying across my skin tight as a band-aid. He dips his fingertips in one of my splashes that landed on his arm. He tastes it on the tip of his tongue then tastes his own splash. They're both just as salty as each other, he says, urging me to taste for myself. I do. He's right. He lets me have his handkerchief to dab the carpet clean. "I'm going to sleep. My body's dead," he yawns.

Same here.

*

What am I to think of God now? I can say my sorry-prayers and have my slate made clean over and over, but how disappointing that becomes. God is disappointing, a weak ruler of the world, another adult I can trick, a parent too easy to get around, one too soft to dish out punishment. Even worse, one who tries to get into my good books by letting me get away with Glenn Shivington touching my cock and me touching his. Guilt is soft too, it barely leaves a bruise inside me anymore, barely an ache to register some sorrow. I have lost respect for God. I say it out loud: "I've lost respect for you, God." Nothing happens. Nothing strikes me down. What controls me if God doesn't? The new itch that controls my body? The bliss of bringing on the wet?

I don't want to be a friend of Glenn Shivington. There can be no friendship with him any more than there could be friendship with a girl I have done private things with. I have done private things with him that I would do with a girl. I could never, after that, have something so slight as a friendship with such a girl. There would be too great a bond between us for mere friendship. I've no feeling of that great kind for Glenn. I only feel embarrassment that he has this secret of our rubbing cocks and comparing the salt taste of the wet. I never want to speak to him again or hear his voice near me or have him brush against me.

He wants to do it again with me, the rubbing. I want to pretend it never happened but he says that when he thinks about our rubbing cocks it makes him excited. He asks me if talking about it as he's doing now makes me excited.

"No," I say. We're lined up for the mini-bottles of milk handed out before school starts.

Why won't I speak to him? he wants to know. He asks if it's because talking to him gives me a stiff. "No," I sneer. "Leave me alone."

He keeps following me, across the playground to the cricket nets to watch the batsman with one pad on, the cork ball's wide V down the concrete pitch from the bowler. In class I refuse him a seat beside me. He passes me a note through a chain of hands. I tear the note to confetti for the bin. Another note is passed. "Everybody does it," the note says. I tear it, chew it into spitball mince for sticking under the desk. Another note: "I've done it with others before. I've done it with Bryce Howe and Ross Quilter." Bryce Howe is sitting in the row over from me. Does he look like someone who would have rubbed cocks with Glenn Shivington? His father's an electrician. Ross Quilter mocks Glenn Shivington behind his back for being a conch and up himself.

As soon as class is dismissed I fling my bag over my shoulder for carrying, deliberately clipping Glenn's head in the process. He shouldn't bandy people's names about, I tell him. He shouldn't have told me or anyone else about Bryan Howe and Ross Quilter. Is that what he's going to do with me? I threaten to hurt him, kill him if he bandies my name about. But he doesn't believe I'd kill him. He doesn't take a step backwards or display the terror I hope for. I'll have to hit him again with my bag to show him I'm not bluffing. I do. I'll have to strike the side of his face with the point of my elbow. I do. He makes a fist, ready to fight me. His thumb is tucked inside his fingers, the fist of someone not used to making a fist. I tell him again I'll hurt him, kill him but it's a hollow threat met with his defiant gaze and amateur fists.

Next class, another note. It reads like a homework essay. It accuses me of being an Ancient Greek. Me, Bryan Howe and Ross Quilter. Ancient Greeks practised their cocks on boys before they were ready for girls. If I don't believe him he has the books that say so at home. The Ancient Greeks were aristocrats, say the books. I however, and the two others, are just boys who can't yet find girls to rub their cocks because *they* are off with older boys. Even if they weren't, I'd be too shy to lay a finger on them or know what to do with a finger.

I no longer want to cheat on my exams with him. I certainly won't be stealing makeup on his behalf.

*

I don't score enough marks for Sydney High but I score twentieth in the grade just the same.

On the last day of primary school Glenn Shivington hands me a letter marked "love letter". I throw it back at him and walk off but he picks it up and runs after me and will not go away until I take it from him and read. The letter says he wants to kill himself. He wants to do this because I hate him and therefore he hates himself. I tell him that nobody kills themselves and I tear his letter in half and flick it into his face. I tell him that I don't care if he does kill himself. He says he intends doing it this afternoon. He's going to jump in front of the three-thirty bus.

"I'll make sure I'm there to watch."

"I love the idea of you being the last person to see me alive."

I say I don't want to give him the pleasure of that and won't watch. He won't kill himself in that case, he says.

"Don't then. Who cares!"

THE NEW BUSINESS IS A STORE in Rose Bay North. Yes, a liquor store though that's hardly a hotel. There's no drinking on the premises for one thing. There's wine tasting, with cheese, which is not drinking, it's *tasting*. Such a *with it* thing to do, says Heels. And I will not be exposed to riff-raff and horis and phone boxes. If Heritage had one Sir Thomas, then it's safe to assume Rose Bay North has dozens. Perhaps not Rose Bay North itself, which Heels herself admits is not so exclusive. But Rose Bay proper. And Vaucluse, which is just down the road and is considered upper crust with a capital U.

And there's Watsons Bay, a little further on from Vaucluse, which is in the same category. These are addresses you really can tell yourself, and anyone else you care to talk to, are *class*. They make people sit up and take notice. This is why we came to Sydney. We really are getting somewhere in life now. "That's what happens when you fall in with the right crowd," Winks has become fond of saying lately, tilting his head up as if telling it to the heavens in appreciation. "This is what happens when you're in the know," he smiles, tapping the side of his nose three times.

He says when you're not in the know you come home from the races with zilch. Zero. But when you're *in* the know, when you're in with the sportsjacket crowd, you go to the races with a $1000 in your kick and you come home with double the amount. Sometimes triple. The sportsjackets know when the plunge is on. Last week Winks had only one bet, but one bet was all he needed: Randwick, Race Five, Windburner, 1000 to 10,000 to win.

That's nothing. Last month his yearling, the one that cost a fortune and was gelded to make him race instead of randy, scored at Rosehill at 33-to-1 when the first three favourites were ridden to lose. That night Winks trampolined on his bed, still in his shoes. He flung handfuls of cash from his body: every pocket of his mackintosh, inside his shirt, down his socks, under his hat. He tossed notes towards the ceiling and they snowed around him. "Yaahoo!" he cried. "Yaahoo!"

"Yeehee!" Heels shrieked, snatching at the money flakes in the air. "Yeehee!" She heaped them in her lap and admitted to being a little too tipsy to count, so Winks helped her bail the money into a pillow slip for morning. They slept with the bulge safe between them.

Next afternoon when I kissed Heels good morning she breathed whisky without waking. Winks snored with a whistle in his nose. I felt under their beds for any chicken-feed. Ten cents, twenty, thirty.

Rose Bay North has a lovely village feel, Heels says to explain away its cramped, clammy untidiness. The smell of mould and decaying wood, a fishy ocean breeze. Drive up the hill of Old South Head Road, its box-flats and shoulder to shoulder box-houses, synagogue like a dark brick cake-building, and there it is, the lovely village feel—fish and chip shop, hair salon, newsagent, fruit and vegetable store, a supermarket. And the liquor store on the corner. Turn right at either Oceanview Avenue or Military Road and you find your way to Kimberley Street and the new apartment in a white rectangle building with brown fringes. The fourth floor, one from the top.

Here the Tasman Sea is my backyard. Its thick scaly tide collides with Rosa Gully below my window. The collision sends up explosions of spray against the cliff. Giant stones have broken off like columns of an ocean temple. The wind is made visible in the form of a whirling mist that blasts my face when I stand on the balcony, then disappears until the next collision, a rhythmical war of rock and water where rock defends, sea attacks. The gully is tufted with scrub and reached from the road by way of a field of green-brown grass, a playfield each evening and weekend morning for a skinny boy throwing a tennis ball to his yapping Sydney Silky and calling "Pee Wee, here Pee Wee" when the dog gets too close to the unfenced edge.

"Why is this suburb called Diamond Bay?" I ask Heels. "Did they find diamonds once?"

"It's Vaucluse," she corrects me crossly.

"Says Diamond Bay on the map," I parry, to annoy her.

"Strictly speaking it's Vaucluse. That's what it says on our mailing address. We're on the eastern and southern fringe of Vaucluse."

"The poor end," Winks jokes, standing in front of the fan with his singlet lifted up. "The bloody hot end."

"The developing end," she corrects again.

"The Jew end. Little Israel," he says smiling into a laugh.

"Don't say such things. You'll put us off the place."

"What a funny lot those Jews are," Winks continues. He takes an imaginary handful of money bills from his pocket and, chuckling as he speaks, tells of Mr Cohen upstairs on the top floor, the Mr Cohen who built the apartment block we're living in and whom we owe a dollar or two in cash—"under the table money" which Winks explains is a system people use when they give you a little discount for buying things, in our case this apartment.

"I hear about these Jews," he says. "And by Christ what I hear is true. The other day when I handed the money over …" Winks licks his thumb and slowly counts the imaginary bills, one hundred, two hundred, three, in an accent that transforms "when" to "Ven" and "the" to "ze" as he explains that ven Mr Cohen counted ze money he never counted ze last bill in ze wad. "'Why didn't you count it, Mr Cohen?' I asked him. And do you know what he replied? He replied, 'Never count ze last bill in case underneaz it zere is an extra bill zat has accidentally been given you which you get to keep for free if it's not exposed.'"

Winks slaps his thigh and cackles. "If it's not exposed," he repeats, and repeats once more.

Heels' eyes are closed with laughing. Tears gather at their corners. "That'd be right," she sighs as her laughter subsides. "They understand the value of a dollar, I'll say that much for them."

Winks' laughing peters out to sighs and one more "if it's not exposed."

"You were in his house?" I ask. Mr Cohen with his olive, Greek-like skin and black mini-cap on his crown? "Would he be welcome in our place?"

"Of course. As long as he didn't try and convert us." Winks' laughter sparks up again. And Heels'.

"Convert us to what?" I ask.

"To his kind," says Heels.

"What's his kind?"

She pinches the top of her nose, dreading having to make an explanation. "Oh I don't know. They don't believe in Jesus or something. Frankly, I'm not interested in explaining it."

Winks chips in with, "They were on our side in the war. They're grateful to us. That helps us get along."

"Why do they wear those little caps of theirs?" I ask.

"Oh I don't know. Something to do with their religion. Let's change the subject for goodness' sake," Heels replies.

"How come Mr Cohen would be allowed through our door but Stephen Papadopoulos or Jonathan Jonathan wouldn't be?"

She groans: "Oh for Heaven's sake." She says the reason has to do with the Mr Cohens of this world are like us. They understand the value of a dollar. That deserves respect.

Winks slaps his thigh again. "They like trying it on, I'll say that much for them. 'If it's not exposed.'"

"That deserves respect. They've got some get up and go those people."

*

The right sort of school will be the one Heels refers to as the "Mansions" at Bellevue Hill. There are only boys at the Mansions, no distractions of girls. How very grand it is, on a grand green hill with a view no one could ever afford to buy unless they had millions, she swoons. Look at that big liner coming through the Heads—a toy boat from this far. You'd swear the water was made of glass. It's not like a school at all but a castle with a cricket field, trimmed garden edges, over-alled men who sweep up leaves. Everywhere you look in every direction there's a very old mansion like in England. "Do you know what it is?" she says. "It's a direct promotion to the hoi polloi. I bet you that's Latin over the entrance. It's like we were in England, right down to you having to wear a boater."

The following code of behaviour is for my benefit. (It's my first day at school. I'm standing in a line of boys on the quadrangle.) My hair: keep it above the collar and above the ears at all times, but no crew-cuts. I must keep my shoes free of scuff-marks. I'm to attend to that myself, not a parent, nanny or maid. The school sergeant inspects the line-up of us all. He stops to blink in my face as if taking a mental pho-tograph. He is very short, a grey-haired old man whose back is so straight it mustn't have shoulder blades, for none form a shape through his clothes. He wears a blue uniform with a strip of colours across his chest like a medal ribbon, like a policeman. A pretend policeman. A policeman of boys. I am to keep my socks held up with elastics and wear my straw boater at all times when outside the school grounds.

I will be expected to wear a kilt on Fridays for cadets which is a kind of schoolboy army. There will be a morning singalong with Colonel Morse who will mount the assembly hall stage in his starched army khakis and shiny Sam Browne belt and lead us through *The Road to Mandalay* and *Pack Up Your Troubles in Your Old Kit Bag* in our loudest voices. There will be chapel on Thursday morning where collection plates will be handed round and the money goes to Africa. I can expect to hear John Lennon's *Imagine* because it's more rele-vant than the old hymns. Any boy who puts an IOU in the plate as happened last week will be caned severely. I will be expected to barrack wholeheartedly for my school at sports events, particularly First XV rugby games, especially home games. And the Head of the River rowing regatta. Supremacy on the water reflects supremacy of the school in general, and the supremacy of the school reflects the supremacy of this tribe of "us". Dismissed.

The definition of "us" seems to be that we are Protestants. There are various tribes within the tribe that's us, but Protestant appears to be the unifying definition. Catholic boys from the Christian Brothers schools or the other Catholic schools are "the other". They're "Tykes".

We, our tribe, us, are mainly drawn from the eastern suburbs: from Paddington to Point Piper. Bellevue Hill itself or Vaucluse, Rose Bay. Or else we are boarders from the country, the bush, with its sheep and cattle stations, its flat brown plains of wheat. These boys have deep sunken eyes that always seem to be in a squint. They have a profusion of freckles and red-tinged hair as if one family bred them all. They keep to themselves this bush tribe and talk about the weather, how there's no rain back home, how the dams are at their lowest level ever. Their speech is a nasal drawl that hardly parts their lips. In their wallets they keep photographs of a favourite kelpie or their father's truck. Though they come from out west do not confuse them with *Westies*. Westies are from the city-west, the factory-west where men work with their hands and not their brains as our fathers are presumed to do even if they're farmers, bush tribers.

Rob Bennett lives in the city-west. He certainly isn't a Westie. His father's a doctor so he's just fine. To be a doctor is the best you can aim to be. The next best is a barrister, the next a solicitor. The best after that is a merchant banker or dentist. The next would be an architect, air-force pilot or army officer, and so on down the list. Which of these professions do you want to enter? asks Rob Bennett. I couldn't say for sure. Which of these professions does your father fit into? he wants to know. None? What does he do? A liquor store? Oh. Does that qualify him as a businessman? I suppose so. That's all right then, he says. A businessman is something.

*

Mr Cohen has a tattoo, pale blue numbers and rough as handwriting on the inside of his forearm. But Mr Cohen is no hori. Mrs Burns has one too and she is clean, neat and wealthy. Her neck is draped in so many chains they form a gold spiderweb on her skin. Gold bangles are stacked up her wrist like quoits. She has so many rings on one finger they make the finger swell as if the blood has been cut off. "How come your mother has a tattoo?" I ask Richard Burns the day his mother works in the tuckshop.

"Why do you think?" he rolls his eyes.

"I don't know."

"You must."

"I really don't know."

"The Holocaust," he whispers.

He does not whisper out of reverence for the Holocaust or his mother who survived it. It's because this kind of talk, Jew talk, can bring a Jew trouble in the quadrangle, in the corridors. There is an Asian tribe at school whose people are sometimes called "slant eyes" or "monkeys". A Jew who brings attention to himself can suffer more than name-calling. Gary

Blackwood from the bush tribe will put his hand up to his nose and mime an elephant's trunk and honk "Jewball. Jewballs are everywhere these days." With Richard Burns he targets his un-Jewish name. "Change your name to one of ours all you like but you're still a Jewball. Hitler was right. If he'd have killed all of you people you wouldn't run the banks and farmers would be better off not having to answer to fucking Jewballs."

Gary Blackwood will punch Richard Burns's arm. He will wrench him in a headlock, knee him in the thigh to make a cork. He will force him to say out loud, "I'm a dirty fat Jewball. Hitler was right." The bush tribe laughs and slaps Gary Blackwood on the back as a congratulation.

Richard Burns doesn't cry when this happens to him. He braces himself in quiet fury, in pain. He doesn't fight back. He is too scared to fight back. He is a first year, a pleb. He is smaller, younger, weaker than Gary Blackwood and has endured one humiliation from him, why risk another by fighting back? He waits for the corking and laughing, the pain, the fury to pass from him like a funny turn, a sickness. I know not to go near him to comfort him in case I'm labelled a Jew-lover, an enemy of Gary Blackwood. Nor does any member of the Jew tribe dare catch the eye of a bush triber or else they will be next.

A prefect comes by. I know it's a prefect by his woollen blue-green tie. He blames Richard Burns for the fighting and warns him, "Next time I'll send you to the school sergeant." The prefect jokes to Gary Blackwood that he should save his knuckles for the regatta.

*

The fifty-dollar tribe is the wealthiest of all. At the tuckshop fifty-dollar tribe people buy a chocolate milk with a fifty-dollar note. The ladies behind the counter have trouble finding change. This tribe's fathers drive them to school in Rolls Royces, Mercedes, Jags. They have pools in their homes though they'd never invite me because their friends have been their best friends since prep school. One day they will invite me perhaps, if I'm persistent. If when the fifty-dollar tribe speaks of Whitlam and his Labor government I agree that they are shaping as a disaster they might invite me. Yes Whitlam is out of control. Yes he is trying to destroy business and the free enterprise system with taxes and union thugs. Yes my parents are seriously considering leaving the country for America or Switzerland as their parents are. Whitlam is out to destroy private schools, the fifty-dollar tribe complain. Where else would people like us go to school? Whitlam wants to ban cadets is the latest word.

Whitlam is a disaster, I agree with them, though I have little understanding of politics. "Your politics is your pocket," I exclaim, nodding decisively. It's what Heels and Winks say if ever the topic of politics is raised.

"Your politics is your pocket," the fifty-dollar tribe repeats. "That's a good way of putting it." What does your father do? one of them asks—Justin Boyce-Harrow. Whitlam wants to stop his father mining in the outback—"I mean it's a desert out there. What else are you going to do with a desert?" He denounces Whitlam as nothing but a socialist: "He'll have us all wearing grass skirts with the Abos."

"My father's a businessman," I answer.

There is a murmur of approval as if I have provided the right password. "What line is he in?"

"Liquor," I reply.

"He might deal with my father," says Justin Boyce-Harrow. "My father has brewery interests. So tell me, does your father own a brewery?"

"He's in all sorts of things."

"In a big way?"

"Oh yes," I say, attempting to sound as proud and superior as Boyce-Harrow.

Another of the fifty-dollar tribe asks if I know the McWilliams people, the wine people. They have a boy who's good enough to play rugby for Australia.

"Oh yes, of course," I lie. "We see quite a lot of them."

I pretend to cough to fend off the interrogation.

Boyce-Harrow pats me between the shoulder blades to help my breathing and continues his questioning. "Where do you live?"

"Vaucluse," I splutter, fending away his patting.

"Good," says Boyce-Harrow. "Since you live in Vaucluse my father can drop you home after school some days if you like. Whereabouts in Vaucluse are you?"

I cough that I live in Kimberley Street.

Boyce-Harrow frowns, "Where's that?" and asks if it's anywhere near Wentworth Road.

I tell him not to worry about giving me a lift home, but he keeps asking where Kimberley Street is: is Kimberley Street that one that runs off Hopetoun Avenue? Is it down near Parsley Bay? Giving me a lift would be no bother at all, his father does it all the time for Vaucluse boys. The fact remains however that Boyce-Harrow can't place Kimberley Street. He's never heard of it and his family has lived in Vaucluse forever.

It's the other side of the Vaucluse shopping centre, I say. Towards the Rose Bay end of Vaucluse.

That's not Vaucluse, scoffs Boyce-Harrow. It's only Diamond Bay.

There are no more offers of lifts home. No more opportunities to denounce the Whitlam government. On the mornings Winks drives me to school I ask him to drop me a long way from the entrance gate, almost halfway down the road, the road of trees, the road of tree shadows and mansions. I explain to him it's so I can get some exercise and start my heart pumping for the day but really it's because I'm ashamed of the Torana among so many fine cars. In fact, from now on I'll take the double-decker bus to school despite the way it bumps and rocks my cock to life so that I have to clench and pinch myself against a stiffie, against ejaculating. Despite having to tramp up the road, higher and higher into its gated hills and then up the steps steep as a ladder between mansions and past the mansion of the old man with no throat, the one who stands on his verandah, lifts up his cravat and blows through a hole in his neck as if clearing a blocked nose.

DON'T BE SO DOWN on everything all the time. Get into the swing of things, Heels says. Give things a go, join in. If the regatta is *the* event of the school calendar then of course you must go, besides it sounds very glamorous, a regatta. It conjures images of very toffy English gentlemen with monocles and ladies with lacy parasols and pretty bonnets. "You'll even be wearing a boater like you're on one of those punting things, punts. A boater is the perfect hat for a regatta," she trills in a sing-song voice, placing it, a thatch of scratchy straw, on my head and setting it square then straightening my tie, smoothing the suit pads of my shoulders. She takes a step back to look at me in my smart grey uniform before farewelling me out the door for the bus to the train station. No she does not know why the regatta is called Head of the River but if that is what it is called then that's what it's called. No need to make snide comments about beheadings and savages with spears. There are no savages with spears left in Australia, least of all on a river at or near Sydney.

But I've heard there is headhunting at the Head of the River. There are headhunters, not so much at the river itself but on the trains going there. It's a secret, that's the rule, that's the tradition. Headhunting is a tradition that's no business of teachers or parents or prefects or police. It's between *us* and the other us's of each school. No one dobs, and if they do, they'll be history, they'll be *got*.

*

The Jew tribe will not go to the Head of the River. If there's trouble, won't they be the first to attract it? Nor can I see anyone from the Asian tribe. Perhaps they fear they would be second.

Throughout Saturday morning the trains pull away from Town Hall Station for Penrith. Carriages crammed with boys and pimply almost-men blazered and scarved in the blues, browns, greys and blacks of their particular school. Each school has its own carriage. On the platform boys assemble excitedly, waiting for their turn to board. They queue, not commanded by anyone to do so—there are no masters, parents or prefects present—but out of some innate conformity.

Gary Blackwood's at the front of my queue. He is jostling us with his elbows to "make room you fucking plebs" as members of the bush tribe arrive. Plebs must give up their place and move to the back of the queue. Carlos Toyne is there—a friend of Gary Blackwood's though not a member of the bush tribe (his father's a chemist at Bondi) but a weightlifter, rumoured to be good at maths all the same. His red scalp shows through his hair from early balding. His shoulders are so hunched with muscle they touch his earlobes. He takes off his blazer and rolls it into a ball for stowing under his arm. He folds up his sleeves into tight cuffs for his hairy biceps, biceps so thick he must hold them out from his body as if carrying bags. He walks a few steps out of our queue towards the neighbouring queue, Enemy One. He sucks in deep breaths through his nose as if preparing to lift a bell-bar. He bares his teeth at Enemy One and gives out a gargling growl, thumps his chest with his fists like an ape, growling louder, hoarser. Veins in his forehead and temples squiggle to life like worms. His eyes bulge in a madman's glare.

The older boys in the Enemy One queue clap and jeer. They mock him with muscle-man poses struck with an effeminate flourish, a bent wrist, a blown kiss. This only makes Carlos Toyne beat his chest more ferociously and roar with strings of spit between his lips. The next Penrith-bound train grinds towards the platform. The school queues burst into song—their school songs—arms slung over the shoulders of the boys next to them. Gary Blackwood punches the air and leads the school anthem. Senior boys, the almost-men who reek of aftershave, those who usually push we plebs aside or to the ground as soon as look at us now fling their arms over our shoulders, hug us to their sides. Even the bush tribe embraces us and does not let us go as the train squeals to a halt. Gary Blackwood has his arm over me and is holding me close. "OK you fucking plebs, let's see what you're fucking made of," he yells. He jerks at the train door to slide it open. Carlos Toyne charges in to claim the empty carriage. The rest of us follow to fortify the carriage, locked in the chain of arms and shoulders unable to wriggle free of the crush. For that's what Gary Blackwood is instructing us to do, "Fortify." We are like his troops now, he is our self-appointed commander.

Carlos Toyne has won the first battle against Enemy One: he has opened our rear door, the one that leads to the Enemy

One carriage door. He has reached across and grabbed the Enemy One carriage door-handle. On the other side, two Enemy One almost-men push against his hold, a test of strength Toyne is winning single-handedly. Whoever wins this contest gains control of the door and will open it, shove an arm through and grab an opponent by the hair, clothes, wrist and drag him through the opening into their carriage. They will have scored a victim.

Gary Blackwood and two bush tribers are gaining control of the carriage's forward door that joins to the carriage claimed by Enemy Two school. Other bush tribers divide the sprawling scrum of us into two packs to lend weight at each door. The carriage's main doors slide shut for departure. The train creaks away from the station, quickly gathers speed and twists double-jointedly on its snigs. Bodies are being squashed in the door-scrums, boaters are toppling to the floor, crushed, there is barely enough air to breathe but everyone is excited nonetheless to be a part of this game. We plebs are shoulder to shoulder with almost-men and bush-tribers. We are honoured to have a role to play, this bond with them, this common cause.

Gary Blackwood yells a command. How many stops till we get to Redfern Station? We must hunt a head before Redfern Station so we can feed it to the Abos. After Redfern Station we must do our best to hunt heads from an enemy carriage and feed them to the Westies at every station we slow down through through the Western Suburbs. He begins a countdown. One. Two. Three. Heave. The two scrums press forward at their appointed doors, plebs in the middle of the pack, bush tribers and seniors behind ordering us to heave, heave, heave.

I'm in the Carlos Toyne scrum being shoved forward while around me other plebs are forced sideways. My arms are pulled backward to the point of dislocation. Boys who a second ago were laughing begin to cry, terrified. *I* am terrified. Hysterical voices scream for the shoving to stop, please, stop because an arm is hurting, a leg, a foot. But the scrums edge on. The Enemy One door is barged open far enough for Carlos Toyne to grip an enemy collar and try to pull it through the gap. Enemy One fists poke through the gap to punch Toyne but he withstands the blows with guttural grunts and refuses to let the collar go. The captive's head is now in the crook of Toyne's arm. He punches the head. A senior boy punches the head and asks a pleb near him if he'd like a turn to punch the head. The boy says No but the senior demands that he does. The boy punches the head weakly. "Harder," the senior says. The pleb shakes his head: No.

Enemy One seniors attempt to pull their boy back into their carriage. They lift his feet off the ground to recover him in a tug of war. The boy's trouser leg rips exposing his underpants. Rips further. The trousers tear from his legs and tangle around his ankles. Enemy One has lost him. Carlos Toyne passes him like a prize over his shoulder onto senior shoulders, onto plebs. The boy's neck-tie is still knotted in place but his shirt has been stripped from beneath his jacket. His underpants are pulled down to his knees. He cups his hands over his privates. Here he comes, passed my way face purple with struggle, cheek grazed raw, blood across his teeth, snot and tears smearing his lips.

"One nil. One nil. One nil. One nil. One nil," the seniors chant. "More weight," Toyne cries as Enemy One counter-surges. My scrum suddenly shoves forward. I'm helpless in its tide. Someone has lost his footing, is sinking to the floor and dragging my section of the scrum down with him.

"Heave, heave, heave," the seniors order.

"Stop, stop," I plead.

"They've backed off," Toyne cheers. "They've backed off. Good job, good job."

The scrum goes slack. At its crumpled sections bodies roll clear. The train jolts, slows. Gary Blackwood calls out, "What station? What station?"

"Redfern. It's Redfern," a voice replies.

Blackwood leaves his position at the Enemy Two door and swims against the tide of his scrum to the centre of the carriage where the captive lies pulling up his underpants. "Man the main door," Blackwood orders.

"Don't, please," begs the captive. Blackwood tells him to shut up and drops his knee into the boy's back and chants, "Redfern, Redfern, Redfern."

The seniors join in, "Redfern, Redfern, Redfern." They clip plebs' arms playfully with their fists to let them know they'd better do what they're told. Everyone must take turns to drop the knee into the captive. "Go on, fucking do it," they command. Blackwood drops his knee again. "That's how you fucking do it," he boasts, grinning. He drops his knee once more into the sobbing captive.

A senior takes a turn. Another senior. A bush triber. Another bush triber. A pleb is pushed towards the captive and made to stand over him and take a turn with his knee. The pleb drops his knee and is made to step aside and let someone else, another pleb, have a go. Another. Then another. Gary Blackwood cheers and applauds them. The accolade spurs others to take a turn and win Gary Blackwood's favour.

I want to win his favour. I want to take a turn. Nothing could be easier than to drop the knee into this pitiful captive and be rewarded with a cheer in my honour, applause. Instantly I would *belong*. But I do not, cannot take a turn. I slip behind watchers to avoid Gary Blackwood catching my eye and singling me out as the next who must drop the knee and prove he belongs.

The train doesn't stop at Redfern Station. It slows to walking pace beside the platform. Gary Blackwood pulls the main door open. He and two bush tribers lift the captive to his feet but he refuses to stay standing. He collapses to the ground, writhing and swearing against being thrown from the train. Blackwood laughs at him and orders two bush tribers to grip the captive they call Scum under his arms and hoist him up and push him onto the platform. "Go," he calls. "Do it now. Quick."

Out goes the captive, sent tripping and tumbling across the platform, his trousers and underpants around his ankles. Gary Blackwood chants, "Boong food, boong food, boong food." He slides the door shut and gives the order for another head to be hunted, this time for throwing to the Westies. The scrums heave at the Enemy One and Enemy Two doors. Three stations later an Enemy Two boy is taken and kneed, his trousers and underpants pulled down to his ankles, his shirt stripped from him before ejection. Soon after, Enemy Two retaliates. It overpowers Gary Blackwood's scrum which is low on numbers because of a need to defend Carlos Toyne's door against a major Enemy One assault. One of the smaller bush tribers is captured. He's fed to the Westies by Enemy Two despite a drive with a beefed-up scrum to capture one of theirs and make a trade.

*

Parents are waiting for their sons at Penrith. They've rugged the high, grassy ground above the river bank. They've laid out a fine spread served from the boots of their cars—roast chicken, lettuce salad, bean salad, pickled onions, breads, crackers, cubes of cheese and flaps of ham rolled like hollow cigars, mustard. They sit on canvas furniture and walking sticks with tops that open out into a seat. They drink champagne from fluted glasses. Their fathers know what's been going on in the trains but say nothing. They were boys once too. They themselves took the same train ride when they were young. They too had to explain to their mothers why buttons are missing from their shirts. Why there are rips in their trousers. Why skin is scuffed from their knuckles, elbows, knees. They too shrugged "I don't know" and had their fathers wink at them knowingly.

I'M AMAZED THEY'RE ALLOWED TO teach Shakespeare and his plays. "Excuse me Sir," I address the master. I've got my hand up. I'm frowning and scratching my head with my other hand. "What is Macbeth meaning in his tomorrow and tomorrow and tomorrow speech? I've never heard anything like it. 'Creeps on this petty pace from day to day' and 'all our yesterdays have lighted fool the way to dusty death'. Life signifies nothing, is what he seems to be saying."

The master replies that Shakespeare is saying that life has no meaning and all human endeavour is futile and sheer vanity. It's a sobering notion, the master admits, it's a philosophical jolt to one's system.

"It's like a suicide note," I say.

"It is indeed that," says Sir.

"Just as the to be or not to be speech in *Hamlet*?"

"Indeed."

Shakespeare is saying there is no God? He's saying that the hope the bible offers—an afterlife, a whole series of second chances that give you every opportunity to get into Heaven—is an illusion?

"Effectively," says Sir.

That means all the study we do in our lives, all the learning of rules and manners, maths, parade-ground marching for cadets, it all signifies nothing?

"Yes. Ultimately."

I contemplate the pointlessness of reading books, learning geography, preparing for a career, for an adult life when a great playwright and philosopher such as Shakespeare has reached the conclusion, albeit once removed in the form of play characters, in this case Macbeth, that all our efforts and days amount to nothing, futility.

I might as well get it over and done with now, my death. I might as well bring it on myself and short-circuit the futility. The next time something goes wrong, the next time I'm confronted with a trouble I consider insurmountable, I will commit suicide. It's a comforting thought. A relief. I have the ultimate power over my destiny with this thought. I lie awake at night and pretend to be dead. I hold my breath, close my eyes, feel my face slacken over its bones. I hear with my mind's ear Heels and Winks grieving for me, see the peoples of the world stop their petty routines in cities, in deserts, despairing that I've departed this earth.

How would I kill myself? There are only so many ways that I, a boy, an almost-man of fifteen can take my own life. I have no gun. I could ask Winks to buy a rifle so I can join the school shooting team as a cover. That's something to keep in mind though the urge to kill myself is likely to come over me so quickly, much too quickly for the rigmarole of joining a team, buying a rifle, learning to load it, cock it (if rifles are cocked)—*Fire*. Too long a procedure.

Of course, there are trains and cars and trucks to jump in

front of, but that would be unfair to the driver, that would make an innocent man a killer. Hanging myself with a rope is an option. Rope is cheap—my bedhead money would be more than enough to pay for it. There are hardware stores everywhere for the buying of rope. The bathroom curtain rod would break under the strain of me hanging from it. The balcony rail? It's a possibility. The school's rugby goalposts on the main oval, or the trees behind the scoreboard, would provide the perfect purchase as well as witnesses, plebs, seniors, the whole tribe of us, to make me more famous than any honour board.

What about poison! Poison would allow me to die in my own bed. But where would I get poison? The school science laboratory. Heels' pill drawer. Yes, it's comforting, it cheers me, my dying. But there is no need to die today, a Sunday morning, a day of do-nothing. The sun lies in silver flakes over the sea. The air on the balcony where I eat breakfast toast is cool and blowing soft on my skin. The boy who throws a tennis ball for his midget dog to fetch is out on the green at Rosa Gully. He tosses the ball straight up, high, high until it loops back down. Up goes the ball again and with it the dog, its stumpy legs dangling in mid-air like a circus trick. Three times the dog catches the ball on its way back down. Four times it fails, the ball bouncing off its snout and across the grass. Now it fails once more, the yellow ball arcs towards the edge of the cliff and the dog barks after it. The ball bounces to the cliff face. To the very edge. Over the edge. The dog scampers and yaps after it, over the edge. "Pee Wee!" the boy screeches and sprints to edge. "Pee Wee," he pleads, and runs over the edge. His echoing voice rebounds once around the rock walls then the gully resumes its flops and gushes of ocean below. A thin mist swirls.

I grip the balcony rail, eyes shut, thinking, thinking: have I conjured this in some imagination place inside the eyes? Somewhere in the neighbouring apartment block a woman is shouting "a boy, a boy". A man, tea-towel and plate in hand, his shirt off, his belly round as pregnancy, steps out onto his balcony. He points down to the cliff and beseeches someone inside his apartment to believe him, believe there really was a boy there and he ran over the cliff.

I hurry into the lounge room to the phone, pick up the receiver, but put it down straightaway. I go back onto the balcony to blink and be certain. The tea-towel man calls across to me, "Did you see him?"

"Yes. I saw. I saw," I reply.

"Has anyone called someone?"

"I don't know."

"My wife's doing it now. He just ran off the edge. Ran right off. The damndest thing."

*

Ask this lad (me) here, the tea-towel man says to the policeman who is taking details, his notebook open on the roof of his car. "A boy just ran over the cliff. The damndest thing." I nod that the tea-towel man is telling the truth. Abseilers crab-walk backwards over the cliff and swing out and down to the rocks below. A stretcher with straps and pullies is lowered. The wind has come up. Spray drifts out to sea like steam. People from the gully's homes stand cross-armed. They curve their hands through the air to describe what happened: one hand for the dog, one for the boy. Then they stand cross-armed again. On balconies, binoculars flash sunlight as if taking a photograph.

A woman in a nightie sits on the grass beside an ambulance, her head buried in a man's embrace. Her back shudders with weeping. A prancing dalmatian barks and lunges at a labrador and is told to get out, go home. The tea-towel man throws a pebble at it. Two children in pyjamas play tag then climb onto the fire engine to which the abseiler ropes are tied. They are told to get out, go home. They jump from the fire engine and run playing their tag.

It's an hour before the winching begins. The men of the gully haul in time after the count of three. I haul on the end of the line. The stretcher ropes squeak on their anchor somewhere in the deck of the fire engine. Here he comes now, up he comes. He is tucked into his puppet-bed in a black sheet of polythene. We step forward to glimpse. His mother is helped forward. Her shaking fingers pry at the polythene exposing his face, a face my age, a face without a mark on it, pale and blue with half-closed eyes and mouth.

Heels is here to fetch me. I shouldn't just stand around and gawk like that, she reprimands. It's a terrible thing that has happened but gawking isn't going to help. "It's a place of death now," she complains marching me home. "I'll never be able to look out from my balcony again. My lovely view is spoiled forever."

She decides a little breakfast jolly-up is called for, a glass of champers and orange juice as if we're celebrating. Such an awful start to a Sunday but there's no need to have the whole Sunday ruined. She closes the curtains so she doesn't have to look out onto the spoiled beautiful patch of green and the spoiled ocean and the spoiled rocks. She tops up her glass and mutters that the dead boy must have been a silly boy: "I'll grant you there was no fence there, but what sort of boy throws a ball over a cliff!"

"He didn't. It just bounced," I correct her.

"It's his own fault," she says, staring resentfully at the drawn curtains.

Her sulky indignation disgusts me, her cheeks flushing with the drink. But one part of her ramblings is true: the gully is now a place of death. And having seen death, a human death, my first human death, the fantasy of my own end, my suicide, my last resort, peaceful, proud, is spoiled like Heels' view from the balcony. How alone it looked, death, dragged up from the blind ocean and rock, a pale and blue face so blank even a weeping mother's fingers couldn't reach it, wake it. Shakespeare's suicide notes do not mention this. He speaks of sleep perchance to dream. But where was the sleep in this? Where were the dreams?

*

All is not lost for the day. Heels has made a plan. We've been invited to Genevieve Plant's for afternoon drinks and nibbles. Is Mr Hush Hush going to be there for once? I ask. Of course he won't be there, says Heels irritably. But why won't he be there? I ask. He's never there. Why not? I know very well he's never there when Genevieve has visitors. That's his policy. But I'm in the mood to argue out of disgust at Heels—those curtains being drawn on such a sparkling morning against a horrible death; that faint slurping sound she makes when she sips daintily from her glass; the clink of her teeth on the rim. Yet I'm no better than her. A boy has died and I feel no pity, no sadness other than for myself for my loss of death as a comforting companion.

Mr Hush Hush's policy is absurd to me, I say. If she, Genevieve, is his mistress—"That's the word, isn't it?" I hiss to Heels who titters "Yes, I suppose that's the word to use." If she is his mistress and it's common knowledge around the traps, and she has a son, Brett, to him and sends him to prep school at the Mansions as he would any other son, then why all the secrecy? Why not be open about it?

That's not how it's done. That's not how the situation is dealt with when you're one of the hoi polloi. Mr Hush Hush has a wife. His wife knows of the Genevieve affair. But he's hardly going to leave his wife because for one thing she is a very wealthy woman in her own right and very well connected. She's unlikely to leave him because he's a very respectable Judge, and who wouldn't want to be married to someone so high up in authority as him? Besides, the old girl's Catholic, so they have a little arrangement: Mrs Hush Hush knows about Genevieve, Genevieve knows about Mrs Hush Hush. Mrs Hush Hush knows about Brett but Mr Hush Hush doesn't rub the old girl's nose in it by waltzing about town with Genevieve on his arm or treating the apartment he set her up in like a second home where friends can come and go for parties like a normal home. Mrs Hush Hush would not be amused.

The apartment—a two-bedroom whitewash two floors up above Old South Head Road at Watsons Bay—is in effect Mr Hush Hush's second home. "He stops the night two or three times a week to see Brett and … and … do what you do with a mistress," Heels giggles, wagging her fingers as if reprimanding herself for saying this.

"Why do you have a friend who is a kept whore?" I sneer. Heels straightens her back in alarm and swallows her mouthful of drink with a loud gulp. "That's what she is," I say. "Do you envy her her glamorous lifestyle or something?"

"I certainly do not," says Heels, placing her hand over her throat in shock.

"Aren't you afraid she might try and play up with your husband?"

"I hardly think so," she relaxes. "He's a bit out of her league. Up against a Judge."

"Are you saying my father isn't good enough for a kept whore? What does that make *you?*"

"Don't you dare call Genevieve that awful word, that *whore* word. She's a lovely person. And I tell you this, she's a very talented hairdresser. Just look at what she's done for my hair." She pats the peach-tinted do on her head. It is wound into her favourite cone-style, a candy floss of hair higher than ever before, twinkling sugary with hairspray. A do she wraps in a turban of toilet paper and hairclips at night to keep it in place. Winks cups its length in his hands and helps lower it onto her pillow like a baby.

"Must be impossible to sleep with that pile on your head," I say.

"You get used to it. That's why your father and I sleep in separate beds, so as I can spread out and he doesn't roll onto Betty." Betty being the name she calls the do because since she spends so long in the mirror with it she might as well talk to it like a friend, therefore it might as well have a name.

"You've lied to me in that case. You said you had single beds because of the old man's heart, so his heart wouldn't get all scrunched up and kill him. He only had five years to live

I was told and that's why I had to be well behaved, because our time together was going to be so brief."

She lets out a dismissive spurt of air through her lips, then smiles and sips her drink. "Well I suppose we said that. But you know ..." Her sentence peters out.

"No," I raise my voice. "I don't know."

She raises her voice. "We said that to make you appreciate us a little more and do right."

The bathroom door opens and Winks steps out, newspaper under his arm, leaving behind him the sound of the toilet flushing. He's tucking his singlet and shirt into his pants. "What's the story here? What are the loud voices all about?" he frowns.

I ignore him and move straight on to my next topic of argument. "Why don't we use Mr Hush Hush's real name when we speak about him? Does anybody know his real name? What is his real name?"

"For our purposes it's Mr Hush Hush," says Heels. "Frankly I don't know his real name."

"Does anyone call him Mr Hush Hush in his presence?" I ask sarcastically.

"That would be ridiculous. I've never actually met the man."

"I wonder if Brett calls him Mr Hush Hush?"

"Now you're being stupid."

"I'm going to ask him."

"Don't you dare."

"I definitely am going to ask him," I insist. "I'm going to ask Brett what it's like to have a kept whore for a mother and how it feels to be the bastard son of a kept whore."

Heels jumps to her feet and points her finger at me that

I'm to do no such thing. Winks says if I use that kind of insulting language in the boy's presence, or Genevieve's too for that matter, he'll clip me so hard. He grips his belt buckle as if to draw it against me and tells me I'm not too old or too big to be given leather across my hide. If I feel this way, if I've got this attitude to Genevieve then to hell with me, I shouldn't come to her place. Who'd want someone in their presence who talks rudely as I've just talked, spoiling the party.

*

But I do want to go to Genevieve's. She's no longer the woman she was, she admits that herself. I never knew Genevieve when she was the woman she once was but she doesn't mind boasting that when she was that woman she would put today's girlies of the racecourse to shame. She was the girlie of the girlies. *Now* she has to dress up and be a glamour puss. She wears furs to turn heads but the heads she turns are other women envying her the furs. But back *then*, back when she was at her peak, she didn't need furs, no siree. She put it all on show and didn't dare cover her god-givens, even in winter. Now she has to apply makeup like a surgeon. She must dye her roots or the blond goes to blazes. And sit-ups. So many sit-ups. Her cleavage is going to jelly before her eyes. "I hate the young," she curses through clenched teeth. "Hate them, hate them. That's my mantra."

But when she's with me, just me, out of earshot and eye-shot of everyone, she apologises. "I don't mean *you*, hand-some. No, no, no. Not *you*." She curls my hand in her hand. "I mean, the new batch of girlies with their wiggles in all the right places. They'll know what I mean when they're forty. But look at you," she says squeezing my hand. "You're quite the beautiful boy, aren't you! Flesh all firm, and that nice, brown, tight skin you have." She strokes my arm in one long sweep. One sweep across my hair. One across my cheek. She hooks her finger over my shirt's top button. "Look at those little hairs coming out on your chest. That's very masculine but not overly so. We women like that." Then she waves her hand. Waving away the spell that has come over me? She asks me to pop another cork of champers and give everyone more drinks. I've learned to hesitate at this point, not to move off and start uncorking bottles at that instant, but hesitate, a second, two seconds, in case one last sweep from her red-tipped fingers comes my way, a soft graze of her palm. And if it does, there's a stare from her that comes with it, such a lingering hold of eyes on eyes that I'm sure she longs to tell me something, is about to say something very important but she never ends up saying it. And as she's in the process of this, this not-saying, an electric sting flares across my skin. My blood misses a beat. When it beats again the throb is so loud in my ears that I can't believe *she* can't hear it too.

I never return the sweep of her hand with my own gesture, my own hand-sweep. Why not? Why am I not bold enough to do it? Would I be welcome to do it? Today I am determined to do it. In that moment between the last sweep of her palm and her stepping away to her guests, that's when I'll do it. Often, when the party's over and it's time for us to go, she pecks me on my lips lightly as she might a relation. When it's time to go today, if she pecks me I'll peck back harder than lightly, and longer.

Yes I want to go to Genevieve's. Of course I want to go to Genevieve's.

What will I wear? What would Genevieve like me to

wear? I scratch my chin to decide for her what she would like to see me wear. My chin is brushy with whiskers. My jaw has sprouted shoots from a shaving ten days ago. I must scrape my face clean with Winks' safety razor though it makes the tops of three pimples bleed. I must shower, swipe deodorant under my arms, dab on Winks' stinging cologne. For my shirt I will wear the crimplene T-shirt that clings to my ribs and moulds well to my chest. I must not let on that I'm making this effort for Genevieve. I must complain about having to socialise today of all days with death still fresh beyond the balcony. I must complain at having to shave, at having to wear a piece of clothing such as the crimplene T-shirt which has a label that digs into my neck in an unbearable way.

"You scrub up well, and smell very nice indeed," Heels remarks sniffing the air as I walk past her up the hallway.

Winks says it's a proud moment when a son starts to use his dad's razor.

*

Aunty Dorothy received a speeding fine on the way to Genevieve's. She has removed her slouch hat arrangement to fan herself, not from heat, from embarrassment, the outrage, the humiliation of being pulled to the side of the road by a siren, spoken to like a naughty schoolgirl, and breathalysed like a common criminal, told to stop her complaining and just blow. "Not a skerrick of alcohol was in my system," she wants us to know, fanning. She's going to write to the Premier. How dare they pull over innocent, tax-paying women.

Winks is boredly admiring a classic ship Mr Hush Hush gave Brett to glue together for his birthday. A woman I've never met before, named Prue, has had a terrible experience this week. "Tell us about it by all means," Heels reassures her half-heartedly. "You're among friends. I'm sure there's a laugh in the story somewhere." Prue, darkly tanned, skinny, wrinkly, begins her tale but her voice soon becomes shrill and unintelligible, a bird chirp of tears.

Heels calls Genevieve from the kitchen to deal with the bawling guest. And here she comes, my Genevieve, gold hair riding her shoulders in rhythm with each stride. White pant-suit, loose, see-through to the bra. She informs us that last week Prue's husband flew from a conference in Chicago and he sat with some tart on the damned aeroplane and by the time he'd touched down at Mascot he'd decided to leave Prue and shack up with plane-girl.

Genevieve kneels beside Prue, takes the sniffling woman's hand in her own. She leans forward and kisses Prue as you would to comfort a child, on the forehead. As Genevieve does this, this leaning forward, caves open up in her blouse between the buttons. I can see a breast muzzled in its bra like a snout. Suddenly she turns to me—did she catch me peeking? "Honey," she smiles. "Do me a favour. Go fetch a wet flannel and bring it. And check on Brett at the same time."

I nod Sure and go to the bathroom.

"I wish he'd move so quick when I ask him to do things," Heels quips.

Brett lies on his bed, knees up, matching the pieces of a new toy ship to a blueprint on his lap. "You OK, Brett?" I ask, trying to sound like a kindly elder. But I don't care if he's OK other than to hear him answer Yes, which he does, releasing me from my obligation.

Genevieve's bathroom is beside her bedroom. I never pass her bedroom without slowing my gait for a look in on her vast frilly bed, its blue, frilly eiderdown, two black, knitted golliwogs with red-button eyes propped on the stack of pillows. Reflected in her wall mirror, her black nightie hangs behind the door. A waft of pot-pourri: orange and cinnamon. This is a room where she is naked. This bathroom is another. Her skin when she's undressed would smell of these scented soaps. I run water from the shower tap to wet a flannel, a flannel that must have washed her body. I lift the cane lid of the laundry basket. Boy's school shorts and socks. Beneath them, stringy lace underwear. A bra, white with fake-flower edges. I press my fist into the mesh cups where her breasts have been. A damp towel, hers surely, so feminine with its flower-patterns and yellow. I breathe her in, the spices from her female bottles.

"Here's the flannel, Genevieve," I say.

She inhales and sighs out cigarette smoke and says, "I can tell you all because you're friends. It's not what I bargained for, this life. I'm cooped up here. I'm so bored hanging around at a loose end now that Brett's at school all day I could scream."

She lays her cigarette in a groove of the ashtray. Smoke from inside her pours from her mouth. I move closer so it drifts across to me, into my face, into my mouth. She places the flannel over the sniffler's eyes. "Mr Hush Hush is saying he'll buy me my own salon, so that's something to look forward to I guess."

Genevieve isn't drinking enough. By now she should be waving her wrists about flamboyantly. Normally she'd be grabbing anyone's hands, *my* hands, for an impulsive dance every time she passed my way. She'd be preparing food in the kitchen, sipping from her glass, chopping food and taking longer than food should take to serve because she's working to the pace of the drink, the numb and drag of gin and wine. She'd be calling for me to come stand here by her and help. Stand here and be good company.

It's this sniffling woman and her troubles causing it. If it wasn't for her, Genevieve might already have begun to lean against me in the kitchen, light-headed and dreamy. How lucky she is to have such a strong young man to lend a shoulder, she'd be saying. Not a boy any longer, a young man. She'd roll fiddly bits of ham and cheese and baby tomatoes into balls inserted with toothpicks. My fingers and hers would touch as I did the toothpick part and she the rolling. We wouldn't be at the arm-stroking stage nor the hair-sweeping stage yet. That is still a way off. We would not be anywhere near the eyes-lingering and blood-banging stage, though these stages would be reached soon enough. Perhaps today will be the day when she says, "Have you got a girlfriend?" I'll lie that Yes I have. What would she think if I said No? Would that make me more of a boy to her, less of a young man? A No signals I'm available. Which answer would lead her to ask directly, "Have you ever had sex?"

"Yes," I will lie. Yes I've had sex. It's not all a lie if you count Glenn Shivington. But Glenn Shivington was only a he. Yes or no, the fact is, the word would have been spoken. *Sex* spoken, crackling and sparking with possibility. There could be no mistake once that word is set loose. Eye-linger and hair-sweep from her would be her sex-signal to me. Eye-linger and hair-sweep from me would be the signal accepted, the signal returned. She would say … what exactly would she say? She will say, "Meet me here tomorrow at midday, or at three or five when Brett is out with Mr Hush

Hush. We will be alone tomorrow." She will smell of scented soap.

I stand in the kitchen and wait for her. Five minutes pass. I lay out bread slices to prepare for the making of club sandwiches. I wash baby tomatoes under the tap. Fifteen minutes. I take ham from the fridge, the cutting knife from the drawer. Finally she arrives, annoyed about what a drama it is, what a disaster of a drinks party. She moves close to me and pats my arm. Not a stroke or a gentle squeeze but an ordinary Thank You pat for making a start on the food though there's really no point in food now because no one is really in the mood. Aunty Dorothy is taking off to begin her letter to the Premier. Prue is staying the night here on the sofa because "We old girlies have to stick together through thick and thin." Genevieve walks away towards the kitchen door. "Your folks are getting ready to leave too," she says.

If I stay still, if I don't acknowledge her, she might come back to check on me. She might at least run her palm down the side of my cheek and say she's sorry we haven't had time for a nice chat today. Her doing that would give me a chance to turn and face her in eye-linger position and reach out my hand and touch her cheek and not take my hand away but leave it there for as long as the eye-linger lasts or I hear the clip-clip of someone's shoes on the floorboards leading to the kitchen.

Genevieve stands in the doorway. "I said your folks are heading off." I nod that I heard her. "Is everything all right sweetie?" She moves my way. She's here, she's back with me. Her long warm hand rests against my arm skin. "Are you all right? You look pale."

I take a step closer to her. A frown has puckered her green

eyes, puckered her brow. She applies the backs of her fingers to my forehead. "You're sweating. You're all clammy." She takes my hand in hers. "And look at you sweetie. You're shaking," she says worriedly. She feels the temperature on my cheeks, one cheek then the other. There is no eye-linger from her but I touch her face anyway, my palm exploring her jaw, the soft give in the skin on the side of her neck. I keep my hand there though her frown has reversed. The flesh has been pulled tight into lines down her face beside her gaping mouth, her globe eyes. She snaps her hands to her sides. She cranes out of my reach. She walks briskly out of the kitchen. Blood drums so hard in my ears I can barely hear Heels calling for me. She's calling for me to come home.

Genevieve won't look at me. I'm about to leave but there's no goodbye peck, no wave, not even a glance. I want to say sorry to her in some way but how can I if she refuses to look at me!

HEELS USES "HOI POLLOI" INCORRECTLY. I've looked up the definition and it clearly states that it's of Greek origin and means The Common People, not the upper crust as she uses it. Nonsense, she argues. We're not in Greece, we're in Australia, and here the hoi polloi are the hoi polloi, everybody knows that. When she says hoi polloi she flicks the end of her nose to mean the hoi polloi have their noses in the air. She shakes her head in a spasm of exasperation. "I hate to think of the money we spend sending you to a toff school and you get *that* wrong."

She concedes that *her* hoi polloi, the crowd she mixes with, the Genevieves, the Aunty Dorothys, is the second rung down. She admits the ones I mix with at that school of mine are the *real* hoi polloi, on another rung altogether. But I'm not to forget who put me in that position—she did, and Winks did. "You remember that," she says. "Don't you forget it."

She hopes *my* kind of hoi polloi aren't as disappointing as her kind. Her kind have begun taking themselves far too seriously for her tastes. Take that so-called party yesterday at Genevieve's. Where was the pleasure in that? One doesn't invite people to a party and then allow a guest to go to water and dominate proceedings with an endless display of the crybabies. "My glass stayed empty for almost an hour. And did we see a skerrick of food? Not a crust. Not a morsel." But most insulting of all in her opinion was the farewell. What kind of goodbye did we receive? None. Not so much as a handshake let alone a thanks for coming and a kiss. "She couldn't get rid of us quick enough, that Genevieve," pouts Heels. "Have you ever seen anything so rude?" she asks Winks. He replies that if Heels feels it was rude then he'll just go along with her view of proceedings, he has no firm opinion one way or the other.

"I don't know what we did to deserve that snub. Have you any idea?" she asks Winks. No, he shrugs. "Have *you* any idea?" she asks me. "You and her were having a right old confab in the kitchen. She didn't let on why?" No, I reply. "It's a mystery," Heels sneers. "You know what I think?" she continues. I hold my breath for an accusation, for a "Who do you think you are? Casanova?" Or a "Here he is, the Romeo for the over-forties." Heels sneers again: "I think I know exactly what's happened. I think she's crossed us off her list. I think she's decided we're not good enough for her. That's what I think. Not good enough even for the second rung down. Not so much as a phone call from the bitch. I'm not calling her. I've got my pride. Though I've got a good mind to ring her and give her a piece of my mind."

Winks wonders if now might be a good time to part the curtains and let the sunshine in. We can't keep having closed curtains on such beautiful days. But Heels is adamant, definitely no drawing of the curtains she yells. She can't bear that death-place down there. That stupid, stupid boy doing that stupid, stupid thing ensuring her special view of the water can no longer comfort her and be a pleasure for her. Winks reckons she needs a breakfast jolly-up. She agrees, resting her forehead on her palm. Yes, she'll feel better after a wine-orange jolly-up that makes her happy instantly. Why, a few of these and she might want those curtains drawn after all, says Winks cheerfully. He places a glass in her fingertips. She sips and sighs, reclines in her chair, closes her eyes and mutters that she might as well be back in New Zealand among horis for all the second rung offers her. At least you knew who your enemies were instead of making friends with people who then turn on you and cross you off their list. The second rung hoi polloi think they're so special, but what about that woman who comes into our liquor store all got up in mink and slips Black Label into her pockets. No better than a dolled-up common criminal. Heels juts and scratches her chair's suede upholstery with her free hand. She spits on the floor hatefully without actually spitting. She tilts the glass to her mouth till it's empty and holds it towards Winks for filling, please. Winks says he'd be happy to.

Heels wants me to tell her about the *real* hoi polloi. The real, genuine article. She sips from her second glassful and is tranquilising into a smiler and sigher. I, her son, rub shoulders with the genuine article every day of the week. I look so lovely in my uniform when I'm catching the bus to the Mansions on the hill. When she sees me she thinks to herself how far she has come in life. "Tell me what the genuine article are like."

I don't know, I answer. I merely sit beside them in class. I don't fit into the bush tribe. I don't fit into the Jew tribe, or any other tribe for that matter. I merely go to school and come home and don't fit in with the genuine article.

"But aren't you going out tonight with a group of them?"

Yes, with the surfie tribe. I'm going to see the movie of Shakespeare's *Macbeth* because we're studying it for English. I understand about the old-style way of the language. The surfie tribe doesn't understand a word. As the movie goes along I'm to translate it for them.

"What's it about, this movie?" she smiles.

"It's about the futility of living and ambition gone wrong," I say.

"Sounds dreadful. Not my cup of tea at all. But at least you're going to the movie with some nice friends from the genuine article. You fit in after all by the sounds of it."

I'd have to peroxide my hair to fit in with the surfie tribe. I'd have to learn to surf and have blue eyes and sun-dark skin. I'd have to learn to steal from shops like they do: bags of chips, chocolates, cigarettes, cigarette lighters. I'd have to creep out of the house at night and try to gain admission to the Sheaf or Royal Oak in Double Bay, and when they won't let me in I'd have to go into the carpark and snap off all the car aerials. And when I got caught, they, Heels and Winks, my parents, would have to pay for the damage. They may even have to bribe the police to keep it out of court.

Heels will not have me talk such nonsense. She's given me the best in life and what do I do? I throw it back in her face by speaking such negative nonsense to spite her no doubt. No doubt I do it to spoil the image she has in her head of the genuine article, she's certain of it. It's not nonsense, I tell her, but she doesn't want to hear my sordid tales. Winks insists I say I'm sorry and promise not to get Heels worked up the way I do with my car aerial talk and police talk and what have you. He pours her another jolly-up and asks if she's ready to draw the curtains.

"Not yet," she snaps. "I'll face the world when I'm ready and not before. It's not every day you get crossed off the list by the second rung."

THE SURFIE TRIBE DOESN'T KNOW HOW it's going to sit through this movie, this *Macbeth*. They want to pay an adult, a stranger, to buy them grog from a hotel. They'll drink it in the cinema, or better yet they won't go to the cinema in the first place, for this won't be like going to the normal movies. It'll be like going to class.

They must always be moving, the surfie tribe. Movement always. Daytimes they find surf where there's no ocean. In the streets there are lawns for a beach, transparent arcs of sprinkler water to squat through on skateboards on concrete waves. There are cracked pavements to paddle down with a slapping foot. But night-times they run to street corners, racing when walking would do. Tonight they push and shove each other into headlocks and spitting. They speak the conversational *fucks* and *cunts* and *shits* of their simple play-anger language. They've broken their names in half into affectionate stub names. Or they've lengthened them by a "sie" on the end to brand each other for their tribe, their "us"—Oggs, Polsie, Jonesie, Coops. They pretend to hide in doorways off Pitt Street like burglars removing their masks. Forget the movie. There are rat-scrapes up narrow alleys, black alleys more like caves you can't see into. There are clattering noises they dare each other to surprise with rushing, stomping, yelling, a kick of rubbish cans. Find a rock someone and bomb the back windows of offices. Follow that lady in a short dress from the strip-club and offer to leave her alone for a feel between her legs.

Shut up and listen. Can you hear that? Can you hear a voice, a human voice up there in the blackness in the alley? "*You* check," Oggs tells Jonesie, nudging him in the back. "You do it yourself," Jonesie replies. "Let *him* do it. Let *him* do it," says Jonesie urging me to go forward towards the voice. The streetlight throws yellow only so far. It's impossible to see past the yellow into the black except for a few beret-lids of the rubbish. A man is in there somewhere. He's cough-singing *When Irish Eyes Are Smiling.* The tune is recognisable though the words themselves trail off to forgetful dum-de-dums.

"Go tell him to shut up," Jonesie says to me. The rest of the surfie tribe agrees that that's what should be done. Someone should go in there and tell him to shut up. Do it for fun. I should be the one to go in, the translator man. But why? I ask. "*Because.*" They say no more than "because" as if the reason's too obvious for explanation. "Why?" I say again. Jonesie says it's because the old dero's an old dero and we can so we should. Polsie yells into the dark: "Shut up you old cunt." But the singer doesn't let up with his Irish Eyes. "I said shut the fuck up you old cunt," Polsie yells again.

They shove me forward. I take a few steps out of the yellow towards the singer then turn around, turn back. Polsie is waving me to get going and see if the dero has any money on him. He might have some money and if he does then we're entitled to it by rights of, well, we're here in numbers and he's just an old dero who'd piss it away anyway.

I don't move. The surfie tribe sneers that I'm a fucking coward. If I had any guts I'd go see if the old cunt had any money. I say that he's just a useless old cunt so let's just forget about him, leave him to his bottle. The surf tribers call me a coward again. A fucking chickenshit coward. They say the dero's so drunk he wouldn't be able to stop me taking his money. Suddenly Polsie pushes past me calling me a chicken-shit coward. He crosses from the yellow to the black and disappears into the alley-cave. The rest of the surfie tribers cross into the black to follow and see what he's going to do. I cross into there too.

My eyes adjust and I make out a human silhouette: the dero wrapped in an ankle-length coat like a blanket, a tent of cardboard over his legs and stomach. He's lying across the alley with his bushy head kinked against the wall. A thud, a flat beach-ball thud of Polsie kicking the cardboard. Now he's bent forward, legs spread as if making a cricket appeal for Out directly into the dero's face. He chants mocking laughter at the dero: "Ha, ha, fucking, ha …" The dero wakes from his song and pulls his knees under himself for protection because Polsie is kicking his shins. The surfie tribers are laughing and turning their heads away because they know they shouldn't look even though they want to. I too look away. If I laugh now I'll be confirmed as worthy of this tribe. The tribe is waiting for me to laugh with them and belong to the transgression. But I already belong to the transgression. I haven't said anything to stop it and therefore I belong. The tribers want more. They slap my back and push me play-fully with their forearms to get me to laugh and take Polsie's kicking and chanting in good humour. I laugh. A forced, false laugh, but a laugh all the same. That makes the tribers nod and put their arms around each other's shoulders, and my shoulders.

I'm included. I resist being included: I don't raise my arms to their shoulders. But there's no denying I feel privileged at this moment to be included in this wrap of arms despite what is happening in front of me, the thing I know is wrong but do nothing to stop. I should unwrap myself. Fine words should be forming in me, a speech to confront the surfie tribers, silence them into guilt. "That could be our fathers," I want to say, but I don't want to sound weak and have the tribers' mouths fart ridicule at me and the notion that their fathers would ever be deros.

Polsie groans and cries out "Fuck." The dero has kicked him, flung a bottle at him. The dero is yelling for his cardboard to be left alone. Polsie has fallen over, shocked at the retaliation. The surfie tribers stop laughing. They want to help Polsie but are frightened to go closer to the dero who now gathers the cardboard around himself like a prized possession. Polsie grabs the edge of the cardboard and tears a piece off. The dero keeps gathering it up though Polsie rips more pieces. Oggs tells Polsie to leave the dero and come away with us but Polsie ignores him and kicks at the dero, kicks at the cardboard. Jonesie and Oggs each take a side of him and pull him out of the alley into the yellow glow and the passing headlight beams of the night's traffic. Oggs thinks the dero's following us so we run up Park Street towards Hyde Park, glancing behind in case the dero's there. He isn't there. At the park we bend over for breath and Polsie jigs on the spot exhilarated as if he's just won at sport. "I got his cardboard. Did you see? I got his fucking cardboard." He wolf-howls to the world triumphantly. The surfie tribers wolf-howl with him. "Fuck that was good," Polsie pants, then wolf-howls again.

I say goodbye, I'm going to the Macbeth movie. They say not to go to a boring old movie, go with them.

"Where?"

"We'll have another crack at the dero," Polsie jigs.

I twist out of their wrap of arms and leave. The surfie tribers take turns to tell me to "Fuck off, translator man. You're gutless."

*

Most scenes in *Macbeth* remind me of the dero. Duncan was king but that didn't protect him from the Macbeth tribe. The dero was a king in his way, king of his domain, his alley. Cardboard for a castle. I name him Duncan. When Lady Macbeth finds blood on her hands, the phantom blood of guilt—"Out, damned spot!"—I squeeze my hands together and wipe them on my knees.

Is there a church open at this hour? Somewhere to pray for forgiveness and make my slate clean, a holy bird-bath to wash the stain from my hands. Even if there were, God's easy forgiveness is easily betrayed, and therefore worthless.

Tomorrow, tomorrow and tomorrow creeps on this petty pace, says Macbeth, but tomorrow I could go find the dero, Duncan. I will. I'll take the money I've saved that's stuck behind my bedhead. I'll give it to Duncan. It's dirty money anyway—fifty dollars stolen from Winks' suit; ten dollars for being a pickpocket's delivery boy. Five dollars in chicken-feed cellotaped coin by coin. A sixty-five-dollar apology to Duncan, one he can hold and count, eat and drink with.

Next morning I get out of bed at six and take the early-bird bus into the city. I walk up Park Street to find Duncan's alley. Even if it means being late for school I'll find the right alley, the cardboard castle, and Duncan himself rugged in his coat, asleep. I'll wake him with my gift, my apology. If he flinches from me, frightened, I'll reassure him I'm here to make amends for the surfie tribe and my own part in last night's episode.

Duncan's not here. I stand in the alley—I'm certain this is the right alley. The remnants of a crumpled cardboard shelter lie in a doorway. The streetlight is positioned at the alley entrance as I remember it. The rubbish bins have been emptied, their lids tossed aside, but there seems the same number of them as last night. Yes, this is the right alley. I wait for five minutes but Duncan doesn't appear. A man in a white chef uniform, his apron smeared in kitchen wipings, steps from a door for a smoke. I ask if he's seen Duncan, a down-on-his-luck type of fellow with a big coat and whiskers. I say this is Duncan's alley at night. The chef sneers that he's seen dozens of him. He flicks his cigarette, half-smoked, into the air and goes inside. Streams and cross-currents of crowds dressed in their morning best flood the footpaths, veer into offices. School will have started by now. My name will have been called by Mr Vella for French. He'll mark my absence with red.

I search the north end of Hyde Park in case Duncan is bundled on a bench, sleeping, watching. Then the south end. A barefoot woman, black soles, black toes with nails like hooks, sleeps on one bench with a grimy shopping bag of her things for a pillow. I ask her if she has seen someone fitting Duncan's description. She stares blankly into the grass as if asleep with her eyes open.

In the alley a truck has backed up to a door to deliver toilet paper and serviettes. I upturn a milk crate, sit, wait. I stand, walk the streets to find other alleys, but Duncan is in none of them. I return to the milk crate.

It's almost lunchtime before I give up. I take an exercise book from my schoolbag, tear out a page and write.

To the man in this alley last night,

I was a member of a group of boys who harassed and assaulted you here. It was a shameful thing to do. I feel terrible about it and would like you to accept this money—sixty-five dollars' worth of money I've saved—as a sign that I wish to make it up to you some-how. I hope this money comes in useful.

Once again I want to let you know how bad I feel about last night. I intend never to be involved in something like that again.

All the best for the future,

A friend.

I drop the chicken-feed into an empty beer bottle that's near the cardboard. I roll my note inside the sixty dollars' cash and stuff that into the bottle's neck. I make sure the money is poking out just enough to be noticeable and attract Duncan's attention. That is, if it's daylight when he gets to it. If it's night-time he might not see it. And there's no guaran-tee that he'll be the one to discover it. It could be another dero. Duncan may not be the king of this alley at all. There may be a different king every night. Even so, it's all I can think to do. I feel better for doing it. I'm sure I shouldn't feel better so easily. I wrote the letter with my right hand.

WE'RE BACK ON THE LIST. Heels presses her hands together in a prayer-steeple: thank you, thank you, she prays to the ceiling. Thank you, thank you, she blows kisses to the ceiling light, her "little sun" as she calls it since the curtains have been permanently closed. It's been a month in the wilderness but she has just this minute got off the phone to Genevieve and we're back on the list for Melbourne Cup Day. "Wouldn't you know it, without the slightest bit of prompting Genevieve apologised for the debacle of her last party." Normally Heels would have said it's a bit rich taking a month for an apology but under the circumstances she's decided not to press the point. She merely told Genevieve she'd wondered if she, Heels, had put her foot in it in some way. But she wasn't going to press the point, except to say she was a tiny bit hurt, but she wasn't going to go on about it, except to say she'd wondered if she'd eaten with her mouth open or something. But under the circumstances she decided to let the matter rest.

By circumstances she's referring to the news Genevieve imparted to her, how things are not as they should be between her and Mr Hush Hush. In fact Mr Hush Hush and Genevieve's *arrangement* has cooled considerably and is all but kaput. Genevieve suspects he has wandering eyes. If it wasn't for the little matter of Brett, Genevieve and Mr Hush Hush would be an item no more. But that's their business not ours, Heels says. The main thing is we're back on the list and on Melbourne Cup Day she'll be at Genevieve's bash. And I will be too if I wish because the invitation extends to me: "Genevieve's very own words, because you're so helpful in the kitchen," reports Heels. "It's a school day and you have my permission to call in sick because, after all, it's that one day of the year."

I have no intention of going to Genevieve's. How could I face her! The mention of her name slumps me forward as if punctured. The memory of touching her face. Her shock, her recoil. If anything I should write her a note as I did Duncan, post it, put it in her letterbox.

I sit at my desk and begin.

Dear Genevieve,

I'm sorry for my actions. I'm sorry I touched your face in that way.

The apology warps into a defence.

Mind you, you have acted in a similar way in the past, which is what gave me the idea in the first place.

I'm angry now. At her. At myself.

It was just my John Thomas talking.

I rip up the note and flush it down the toilet. An hour later I attempt another. I begin it *Dear Genevieve*, scrub it out for *To Genevieve*. The note is not a note at all. It has become a poem for me to keep in my drawer with my other poems, or folded and zipped away privately in my wallet behind my bus pass like special money for looking at.

Where bouquet of pines so rich with scent,
Where lonely eyes of life have spent,
Where syrup drifts the dozy creek,
Alone again awake to seek.

Unveiled among reflections bright,
Descending hair against moonlight.
When all the stars are knitted above,
The jewels upon the planet's glove.

The last line is my second choice. My first choice is,
I touch your face and say I love.

But as last lines go it's much too corny, and too close to
the bone.

I've done no homework for weeks. A composition is
due for English, but I can think of no topic. I hand in my
Genevieve poem, name changed from *To Genevieve* to *A Poem
for Someone.*

I'm marked seven out of ten. I'm happy with that though
Mr Collins is sure I can do better. He says next time try writing from real life.

No, I will not go to Genevieve's party. I lie awake and
repeat that I will not go to Genevieve's. I imagine Genevieve
phoning us and I happen to answer. "I'll get my mother," I
say, determined not to converse.

"No need," she says. "I just wanted to make sure you *all*
were coming to my party. That includes you. Do, please do. It
would be so good to see you. I apologise for carrying on like
a pork chop, getting all flustered that day in the kitchen."

"I don't know what you mean."

"Oh I think you know very well what I mean. You will
come to my Melbourne Cup bash, won't you?"

I will not go to Genevieve's. I will not. I will not. My gentle, beautiful, rejecter Genevieve.

I will.

WHAT A RELIEF, SAYS HEELS, the sniffling woman isn't here—she's back with her husband. Things didn't work out with aeroplane girl. It's a reasonable gathering in her opinion. Reasonable without being sparkling. Heels can pick out a few faces. A few clothing designers she's seen in magazines, including that what's-her-name who's in that ad on TV. "I hope we haven't been invited simply to make up the numbers," she mutters, and then notices a face whose name she forgets but who's a fill-in newsreader on the ABC. And there's that fellow who looks like Mike Willesee, who *isn't* Mike Willesee but who was in *Number 96* with that blond thing, Abigail. There was a time when someone like Abigail would be here. When Heels doesn't see someone here she thought would be here, she wonders if they've moved up a rung or down a rung. Yes, a reasonable gathering though it's plain to see Mr Hush Hush has tightened the purse strings because that's the third time this year Genevieve has been seen in that calf-skin lace-up blouse number. And go into the kitchen and take a peep for yourself: Genevieve has been spotted secretly filling white wine glasses from a wine cask instead of from bottles. It's beside the refrigerator and covered by a tea-towel. And doesn't she look drawn!

Heels kisses close to Genevieve's face but at a comfortable distance from her makeup and tells her she looks terrific and that there's such a wonderful crowd here, so many Sydney faces. She asks after Brett. Brett's fine and spending the day with Mr Hush Hush on his yacht, *Treading Water*.

Eventually Genevieve leans forward and kisses close to my face then wipes me with her thumb below my ear though I'm sure I felt no graze of lips and lipstick. She doesn't speak to me. She turns and introduces Heels and Winks to a urologist who fixed her father's prostate and his clinical psychologist wife who should really fix all our heads. Heels greets them with the plum in her mouth that she always uses for doctors: "How do you do?"

Winks excuses himself to take up position with a race guide and glass of beer in front of the radio where the big race will come live from Melbourne. He predicts Van Der Hum is a certainty now that it's pouring rain in Melbourne.

It's half an hour before Genevieve says a word to me, and then it's only to ask me to pass sandwiches around the room. "There's a dear." She does however ask me to do this with her fingers curling around over my wrist. She hasn't as yet looked me in the eye. I pass the tray around then place it on a sideboard. I stand beside Winks who is trying to improve the radio reception by turning the antennae more west, north, west, south. I watch for Genevieve, wait for her to speak, to curl her fingers around my wrist again. Is she avoiding me, spending so much time at the other end of the lounge room?

"I'm thinking about heading home," I say to Winks. "Can I have the house keys?"

The keys drop into my hands at the same moment Genevieve places her hand on the small of my back and rubs the hollow there, once, twice, up, down, up.

"You're not going are you, sunshine? I was hoping you'd be a helper in the kitchen. Help me for a second?"

I nod that I'll be pleased to help her.

I stand at the sink, arms folded as if about to be lectured. "What would you like me to do?" Now it's me who can't look in eyes.

"I need to say something," she whispers, tenderly scratching the hair on my arm. "I'm sorry if I bewildered you, or whatever the word is."

"I don't know what you mean," I whisper back, staring at the floor.

"Oh come on. Yes you do. We're talking about last month. I was … I don't know what I was doing. I led you on and that was very bad of me." She lights a cigarette and empties the last of the gin bottle into her wine glass. She offers me a drag on her cigarette. I take it. A sip of her gin. I take it, wincing from the iodine fire.

She whispers some more, "I've been unable to get it out of my mind. And yet I wanted to get it out of my mind because I'm very flattered but … but …" She drags and sips. "Do you think I'm attractive?"

I lock my folded arms tighter and nod Yes.

"Everything with Mr Hush Hush is falling down around me but I've been distracted when I think of you. I don't know whether I mean distracted or heartened or …" She drags and sips some more. We stand there, not looking at each other, but with her passing me the lipsticked end of her cigarette. Out in the living room Winks calls out that the horses are going to the barrier. The radio is turned louder.

Kissing Genevieve isn't how I thought it would be. For one, it isn't taking place in the kitchen. It's taking place in the laundry behind the kitchen with the white squares of washer and wall-dryer to squeeze past. I don't even know who kissed who first. The door slid shut on its rollers and now she stands so close to me she's under my chin. She holds my hands, her fingers pushing between my fingers so that they splay and she can grip and ungrip them deep into the webbing. She looks up and I look down at her, her eyes globed wide. They begin to water and shine. Her breath smells stale of cigarettes and many drinks, her body of soap perfumes. Her lipstick is cracked around her mouth and smeared on her front teeth. She suddenly stops gripping my webbing and flattens her palm against my back's hollow, rubbing it low, down further and over my buttocks, down lower still, across my legs and up. Then she hugs me as if I'm about to leave and she's trying to prevent me, or she's in grief and needs to be held and comforted. She lifts her head so it nuzzles my throat. She whispers, "Please never let Brett know. Never tell." I whisper back that I won't tell anyone. I won't tell at school.

She lifts her bra and I creep my fingers through the frill and soft wire to spongy skin, nipples like wrinkle-raisins. She flattens her hand against my back's hollow and rubs up and down, lower, lower, over my bum and around the top of my thighs to the front where my cock's stiff and hurting to push out of my jeans. She holds it through the material, squeezes and wiggles her fingers into the top of the jeans and onto its head and rim. I'm paralysed by the tingle and icy-burn of her doing it. She groans, butts my neck gently as if beginning to cry a small cry. She grips my hands again and pulls them down to be at my sides and keeps pulling as if she's using me for balance or in pain and pulling on my hands will help. As she does this she parts her legs over my left leg and sits and pushes down on my knee and rocks on it as if riding. She cries again, a half-cry, not real crying but jerky breath-sobs.

She rests her head on my chest. She makes a fist and thumps it limply on my shoulder. Then she pulls away from me suddenly. She shimmies her clothing into place, tightens the laces of her top and surely now is crying for real.

She slides the laundry door open. She walks out, into the kitchen, head bowed. She's coming back to me, isn't she? I'm to wait here, she's coming back?

She leans against the kitchen sink, silent, empties crackers onto a platter, chops squares of cheddar onto the platter, forcing the knife harder onto the board each time—even if I spoke she wouldn't hear me over that. That's the chopping of someone for whom something has happened that must never be referred to again.

Barracking blasts from the living room. A yeah-yeah shouting and cheering. Genevieve shakes her hair from her face and springs on her toes to serve her tray out there quick smart.

"Who won? Who won?" I hear her.

Winks shouts the shouting down. "Van Der Hum won it. I was right. Didn't I say he was a certainty!"

Heels congratulates him as the cleverest husband in Australia. When she gets home she's going to fling those curtains open.